Create Your Own Camping ACTIVITIES

Lonely Planet Kids

ACKNOWLEDGEMENTS

Commissioned and project managed by Duck Egg Blue Limited

Author: Laura Baker
Editor: Kait Eaton
Illustrators: Daniel Rieley and Yu Kito Lee
Designers: Duck Egg Blue Limited and Stephen Scanlan
Publishing Director: Piers Pickard
Publisher: Rebecca Hunt
Editorial Director: Joe Fullman
Commissioning Editor: Kate Baker
Art Director: Andy Mansfield
Print Production: Nigel Longuet

Published in June 2023 by
Lonely Planet Global Limited
CRN: 554153
ISBN: 978 1 83869 599 6
www.lonelyplanet.com/kids
© Lonely Planet 2023

10 9 8 7 6 5 4 3 2 1

Printed in China

All rights reserved. No part of this publication may be reproduced, stored in a retrieval system or transmitted in any form by any means, electronic, mechanical, photocopying, recording or otherwise except brief extracts for the purpose of review, without the written permission of the publisher. Lonely Planet and the Lonely Planet logo are trademarks of Lonely Planet and are registered in the US Patent and Trademark Office and in other countries.

Although the author and Lonely Planet have taken all reasonable care in preparing this book, we make no warranty about the accuracy or completeness of its content and, to the maximum extent permitted, disclaim all liability from its use.

STAY IN TOUCH

lonelyplanet.com/contact

Lonely Planet Office:

IRELAND
Digital Depot, Roe Lane
(off Thomas St), Digital Hub,
Dublin 8, D08 TCV4, Ireland

Paper in this book is certified against the Forest Stewardship Council™ standards. FSC™ promotes environmentally responsible, socially beneficial and economically viable management of the world's forests.

CONTENTS

AN ACTIVITY ADVENTURE	6
WHAT YOU'LL NEED	8

BACK TO BASICS — 11

CAMPING KIT	12
PITCH A TENT	14
CREATE SHELTER	16
SNACK ATTACK	18
FIND YOUR WAY	20
BUILD A CAMPFIRE	22
HARNESS THE SUN	24
MORSE-CODE MESSAGES	26
LOTS OF KNOTS	28
SUNNY TIMES	30

CAMPSITE GAMES — 33

HUNT FOR TREASURE	34
OBSTACLE COURSE	36
WATER GAMES	38
SPORTS DAY	40
CREEPY-CRAWLY BINGO	42
SUPER SPOTTER	44
TOWER CHALLENGE	46
TABLE TENNIS	48
BALL GAMES	50
FAIRGROUND FUN	52

CAMPING CRAFTS — 55

MAKE A NATURE COLLAGE	56
PAINT WITH NATURE	58
CAMPSITE CROWNS	60
STICK MAZES	62
LEAF RUBBINGS	64
BUBBLE FUN	66
MAKE YOUR OWN BINOCULARS	68
WILD WINDSOCK	69
FLYING HIGH	70
WALKING STICK	72
CRAFTS THAT ROCK	74

RAINY DAYS — 99

COLOURING FUN	100
CAMPING QUEST	102
CARD GAMES	104
YOUR ANIMAL PERSONALITY	106
ANIMAL GAMES	107
NATURE YOGA	108
SPOTTING A–Z	110
MUDDY KITCHEN	112
SLIMY SPOTTING	114
RAINDROP MUSIC	116
MAKE A RAIN STICK	117
PUDDLE JUMPING	118

AROUND THE CAMPFIRE — 121

MARSHMALLOW DELIGHTS	122
CAMPFIRE GAMES	124
CAMPFIRE SONGS	126
TELLING TALES	128
STORYTELLING STONES	130
GUESS WHO	132
TORCH GAMES	134
SHADOW THEATRE	136
KNOW THE NIGHT SKY	138
GAZE AT THE STARS	140

ENDLESS FUN! — 142

MAKE YOUR OWN DICE — 144

THE GREAT OUTDOORS — 77

GET TO KNOW TREES	78
NATURE JOURNAL	80
SCAVENGER HUNT	82
MAKE A MAGNIFYING GLASS	84
NAME YOUR FINDS	86
CLOUD SPOTTING	88
FEED THE BIRDS	90
BIRD SPOTTING	91
FINDING FOOTPRINTS	92
BUG HOTEL	94
CREATURES OF THE NIGHT	96

AN ACTIVITY ADVENTURE

Get the most out of your camping **adventure** with activities to make, play and do around the campground. **Go wild** in the great outdoors!

Whether it's sunny or rainy; whether you're on a hike or by the fire; whether you're playing solo or with friends and family, these pages are filled with ideas for you.

Take advantage of your surroundings and be inspired by nature. Use rocks as playing pieces, sticks as paintbrushes and flowers as stamps. Listen to the birds and watch the sky. Use your tent as a puppet-show backdrop, and do yoga under a natural shelter. Switch on your senses, unleash your creativity and let your imagination run wild!

Discover the possibilities hidden around you as you create and play again and again.

The number of campers suggested for each activity appears in the top corner.

If an activity requires any materials to make, you'll find them listed here.

For activities that need creating before playing, follow the 'How to make' instructions.

Your adventure begins here
As you journey through this book, you'll go back to basics, play campsite games, make camping crafts, explore the great outdoors, keep busy on rainy days and gather around the campfire. At the end of the book, you'll find a dice template and even more ideas and inspiration.

LET'S GET STARTED!

CREEPY BINGO

Look high and low and **pay close attention** to the wildlife around you to come out on top in this game that's **crawling** with fun. Make your own playing boards, then see who can be the first to shout '**Bingo!**'.

You will need
- Paper
- Ruler
- Pencil
- Felt-tip pens

How to make

1 Use your ruler and pencil to draw six vertical lines six horizontal lines on a sheet of paper, to create a 5 x 5 of 25 squares.

2 In the centre square, draw a star. This is a free spa that counts as one of your completed squares.

3 In the other 24 squares, write the names of differ insects, bugs and other critters that you might spot aro the campground.

Learn how to play here!

...RAWLY

How to play
Throughout your camping holiday, keep your eyes peeled for the creatures on your board. This might be around the campsite, on nature walks or as you go for a drive. Every time you spot one of the creatures, tick it off your board with a felt-tip pen. The goal is to complete a line of five (across, down or diagonally). As soon as you do, shout out 'Bingo!'. The first person to shout 'Bingo!' wins.

Beetle	Centipede	Fly	Spider	Bumblebee
Wasp	Butterfly	Worm	Ladybird	Grasshopper
Slug	Firefly	FREE SPACE	Ant	Dragonfly
Moth	Frog	Caterpillar	Stick insect	Mosquito
Pigeon	Snail	Blackbird	Squirrel	Dung beetle

Repeat steps 1 to 3 to create a bingo board for each ... on playing. Write the items in different spaces on the ... so that no boards are the same. You could also include ... rent items on each board to make it interesting!

Go beyond bugs to fill your board! What else might you spot?

Bird bingo
Instead of creepy-crawlies, use a guidebook to fill your grid with all sorts of different birds that you might spot on your camping holiday. Look carefully to identify them in the wild (but don't touch!).

Lots of activities give extra ideas and tips for ways to invent your own variations.

WHAT YOU'LL NEED

These activities have been carefully chosen and designed to do **around the campsite**. Many of them involve basic craft materials, natural materials – or nothing at all!

Check the **'You will need'** list of each activity so you know what materials you should have on hand to **make and do**.

Pack prepared
When you're packing for your trip, squeeze in some crafting and activity basics so you're ready for crafts at any time!

Plan to pack:

- Felt-tip pens, colouring pencils, crayons
- Scissors
- Paper
- Sticky notes
- Card
- Glue stick
- Ruler
- Paint
- Pen
- Sticky tape
- Pencil

You can also use camping materials in your activities:

- String
- Rope
- Paper cups and plates
- Bowl and spoon
- Buckets
- Sponges
- Clothes pegs
- Marshmallows
- Washing-up liquid
- Torch
- Timer and camera (you could use apps for these on an adult's mobile phone)
- Recycled materials, such as cardboard, plastic bottles, cartons, empty cans, jars, toilet rolls and ice lolly sticks

Look for other materials around the grounds:

- Sticks, twigs, logs
- Bark
- Leaves
- Grass
- Stones
- Pinecones
- Flowers

Note: Never take items off living things! Find natural materials, such as leaves, on the ground.

THERE ARE NO LIMITS TO YOUR IMAGINATION!

Be creative

Many of these activities are flexible, so make them work for you! If you haven't got what's on the list, look around and see what you DO have instead. Could you use empty boxes such as cereal boxes for card? Stones for playing pieces? Scrunched-up paper for a ball? Get creative!

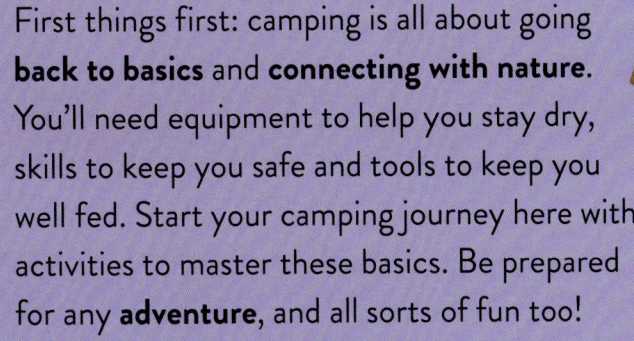

BACK TO BASICS

First things first: camping is all about going **back to basics** and **connecting with nature**. You'll need equipment to help you stay dry, skills to keep you safe and tools to keep you well fed. Start your camping journey here with activities to master these basics. Be prepared for any **adventure**, and all sorts of fun too!

CAMPERS 1+ (PLUS ONE ADULT)

CAMPING KIT

To have the best camping holiday, you need to **be prepared**. Before you set off, **make your own camping list** to help you gather everything you need for the perfect adventure.

ESSENTIALS:

Tent talk
There are all sorts of tents available. Do you need a large tent to fit a family and friends? Or a lightweight frame that you can easily carry with you? Shop around with an adult for the tent that suits you best. Remember that you could buy, rent or borrow. Learn more about pitching a tent on pages 14–15.

Sleeping soundly
You'll need a sleeping bag to stay warm at night. Consider the time of year that you'll be camping and match your sleeping bag to the season. A light one should do in the summer, but if you're camping in the autumn, you'll need a thicker, warmer one. Find a mat or air mattress to place below your sleeping bag too.

Lots of layers
The weather can change a lot through the day, and even in the summer it sometimes gets very cold at night. Pack layers, such as shorts, trousers, t-shirts, jumpers and coats, and you'll be ready for anything! Don't forget a sun hat for sunny days and a raincoat for rainy ones.

You will need
- Paper
- Pen

How to make

1. Write a list of everything you need to bring on your camping holiday. Have a look at the ideas on these pages to get you started.

2. Tick each item on the list as you pack it!

YOU MIGHT ALSO LIKE TO TAKE:

- ✔ Clothes
- ☐ Pyjamas
- ☐ Blankets
- ☐ Raincoat and umbrella
- ✔ Wellies
- ☐ Sunglasses and sun hat
- ☐ Sun cream
- ☐ Swimsuit
- ☐ Towel
- ✔ Toiletries, such as shampoo, soap, toothbrush and toothpaste
- ☐ Insect repellent
- ✔ Plasters and first-aid kit
- ☐ Hand sanitizer
- ☐ Lantern
- ☐ Torch
- ☐ Compass
- ☐ Cooking equipment and food
- ☐ Water bottle
- ☐ Rope
- ☐ Scissors
- ☐ Rubbish bags
- ☐ Guidebook

What else can you think of to bring? Your favourite teddy? Books? Games and outdoor toys? The challenge is to try not to pack too much, but also to make sure that you've got everything you'll need!

CAMPERS 1+ (PLUS ONE ADULT)

PITCH A TENT

One of the first things you should do when you arrive at your campsite is to **pitch your tent**. This will be much easier in the daylight than when darkness falls. Before you go, **practise** putting up your tent in your garden to become a **tent-pitching expert**.

You will need
- Flat, open space
- Groundsheet (optional)
- Tent
- Big stone or rubber mallet

How to make

1 Choose a flat space to place your tent. Clear any branches, stones or debris.

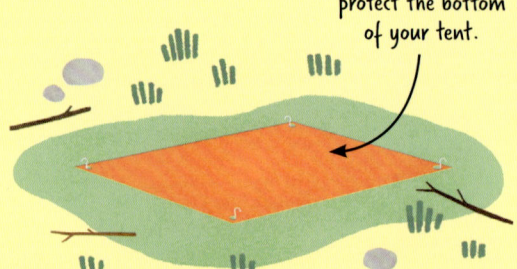

A groundsheet will protect the bottom of your tent.

2 Lay a groundsheet flat on the ground and pull it tight.

3 Follow your tent's instructions to pitch the tent over the groundsheet. Use the poles and pegs to secure it in place. You can knock these into the ground using a stone or rubber mallet.

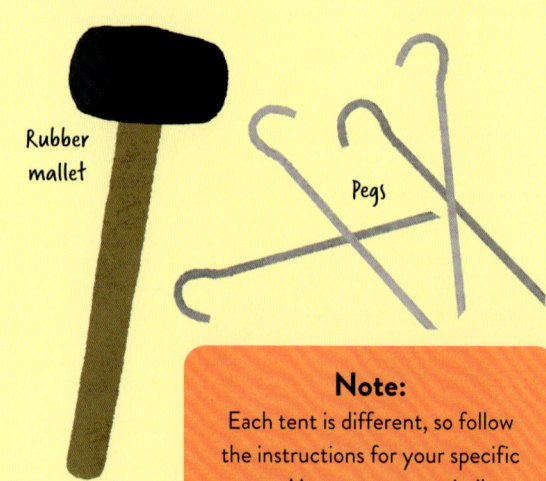

Rubber mallet

Pegs

Note:
Each tent is different, so follow the instructions for your specific tent. Most tents use a similar technique to these steps.

CAMPERS 1+ (PLUS ONE ADULT)

CREATE SHELTER

Your tent is the main base for your camping holiday, but when you venture out **exploring**, you might want to **build shelters** too. Try these different types at home or **in the wild**.

Note: Never take branches or leaves from living trees. Find all your materials from fallen items on the ground.

TEEPEE

You will need
- Long fallen tree branches
- String
- Twigs, leaves and grass

How to make

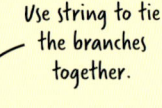

Use string to tie the branches together.

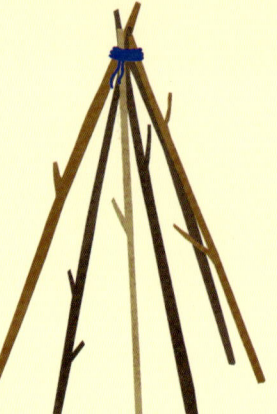

1 Lay about six long branches in a bundle on the ground with the ends lined up. Use your string to tie one end of the branches together.

2 Ask an adult to help you stand up the branches, with the string at the top. Carefully spread out each branch into a teepee shape. Push the ends into the ground.

3 Weave in more branches, twigs, grass and leaves to fill the gaps. Make sure you leave an open area for the door!

LEAN-TO

You will need
- Tree with a low fork in the branches
- Long fallen tree trunk
- Medium branches
- String
- Grass, dead leaves and moss

How to make

1 Ask an adult to help you lay one end of the long tree trunk in the fork of the tree. Place the other end on the ground, so that it rests on the diagonal.

2 Place branches one at a time from the ground up to the diagonal trunk. Tie in place using string. This should create a slanted wall on one side.

3 Weave long grass, leaves and moss through and over the branches to seal the den.

A-FRAME

You will need
- Two trees
- Sheet, blanket or tarpaulin
- Rope
- Sticks
- Clothes pegs

How to make

1 Tie the rope around one tree, just above head height. Pull the rope straight across and tie it around another tree nearby.

2 Hang your sheet, blanket or tarpaulin over the rope.

3 Pull the ends of the sheet outward to form an A shape. Ask an adult to help you put sticks in the ground at each corner. Use a clothes peg to attach each corner to each stick.

Step it up
Have a den-building competition! Set a time limit and see who can build the best den before the time is up. You could make up categories such as cosiest den, most secure, most watertight and more. Then have fun testing each creation.

CAMPERS 1+ (PLUS ONE ADULT)

SNACK ATTACK

If you're going out exploring, you'll want to make sure you have **plenty of food and water**. Pack a picnic and try **creating your own snacks** too.

MAKE YOUR OWN TRAIL MIX

You will need
- Nuts, such as peanuts, pine nuts, almonds and/or cashews
- Sunflower seeds
- Multigrain cereal hoops
- Dried fruit and/or raisins
- Chocolate chips or plain chocolate bar cut into chunks
- Snack pot
- Spoon

How to make

1 Gather together any of your favourite ingredients above.

2 Place a small handful of each into the snack pot. Stir.

CARRY WITH YOU AND ENJOY!

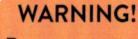

WARNING! Do not use nuts if anyone has an allergy.

MAKE A PORTABLE SALAD

How to make

You will need
- Apple
- Knife
- Spoon
- Bowl
- Cottage cheese
- Chopped nuts
- Raisins
- Cocktail sticks

Bring your salad and spoon with you on a walk. Once you've eaten the salad, enjoy the bowl too!

1 Ask an adult to cut off the top of an apple. Set it aside.

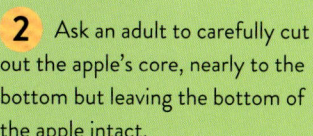

2 Ask an adult to carefully cut out the apple's core, nearly to the bottom but leaving the bottom of the apple intact.

3 Carefully scoop out as much of the inside of the apple as you can, leaving the skin intact. Place this in a bowl.

4 Add two large spoonfuls of cottage cheese, a small handful of chopped nuts and a sprinkling of raisins to the bowl. Mix together.

5 Spoon the mixture back into the apple, until just full. Place the top back on and secure it with cocktail sticks.

FORAGING FOR FOOD

The great outdoors is full of natural treats. However, many of these are not safe to pick or eat. Find a guidebook for your area and check it carefully with an adult to discover wild berries and plants that you might be able to try. Never pick items if you are unsure they are safe.

When you're walking with an adult, look carefully at the plants and berries around you. Can you match them to the same plants in your guidebook? Keep a log of what you find. You could draw your findings too.

CAMPERS 2+ (PLUS ONE ADULT)

FIND YOUR WAY

When you're in the wild, it's important to know how to **find your way** around (and back!) so you don't get lost. Learn to **use a compass** and **read a map**, and make your own map for someone else to follow!

> **You will need**
> - Paper
> - Ruler
> - Pencil
> - Colouring pencils
> - Compass

MAKE A MAP

Design a map based on your campsite and its surroundings. Then see if a friend or family member can use it to find their way around.

1. Use a ruler and pencil to draw a grid on a piece of paper.

2. Draw your campsite first, then work outwards.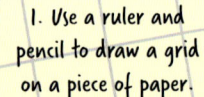

3. Add roads and paths.

4. Add any items that stand out, such as a unique tree, hills, a picnic table or a lake.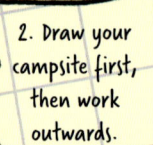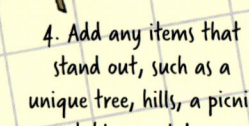

Draw an arrow to show which way is north. Use the tips on the next page to help.

5. You could add a key with symbols to represent different areas on the map.

Key
Campsite
Toilets
Boating area
Nature walk
Water

USE A COMPASS

A compass has a magnetic needle that always points to Earth's North Pole. It can help you find the direction to your destination.

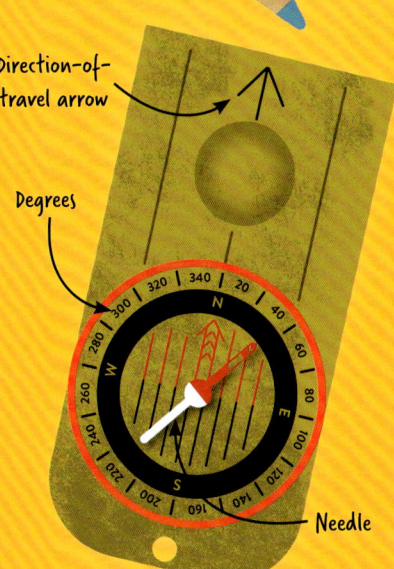

Direction-of-travel arrow

Degrees

Needle

Find north

1 Hold the compass flat in front of you. Let the needle settle.

2 Look at the red part of the needle. This will always point north.

3 Turn around slowly, holding the compass steady. Stop when the red needle lines up with the direction-of-travel arrow marked on the compass. This arrow is now pointing north.

4 Mark north, south, east and west on the map you drew of your campground. Look at which way you're standing in relation to the camp. Ask an adult to help.

Reach your destination

Use your compass to help you find your way by map. Choose a starting point and an end point.

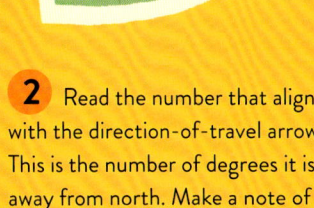

1 Place a map on the ground. Place your compass on the map, with the direction-of-travel arrow pointing to where you want to go. Let the needle settle.

2 Read the number that aligns with the direction-of-travel arrow. This is the number of degrees it is away from north. Make a note of this number.

3 Put the map away. Hold the compass flat and align the direction-of-travel arrow with the number you noted in step 2. Walk in this direction. As you walk, continue checking that the needle is lined up with N and that you are walking in the direction of the degrees noted.

Note:
If you don't have a compass, you can use a compass app on a mobile phone.

CAMPERS 1+ (PLUS ONE ADULT)

BUILD A CAMPFIRE

Light up your trip with a **glowing campfire**. This is useful for keeping you warm and dry – and for **cooking treats** too!

You will need
- Firepit
- Tinder, such as dried bark and hay, or pre-bought fire starters
- Kindling, such as twigs and small sticks
- Matches or lighter (for adult use only!)
- Logs

Did you know?

When building a fire, you need tinder, kindling and fuel. **Tinder** is dry, flammable bits of wood and paper that help the fire get started. The tinder then ignites the **kindling** – small sticks that build up the fire. Once the fire gets going, you need **fuel** such as logs of dry wood to keep it roaring strong.

WARNING! Never build a fire without an adult to help.

Fire safety

- Each campsite has its own rules about where and when you can build fires, so check these carefully. Many campsites only allow fires in designated firepits.
- Build the fire in a clear, open, outdoor space. Never light a flame inside your tent.
- Look out for overhanging branches and trip hazards.
- Never leave the fire unattended.
- Be sure the smoke will not blow into your tent or someone else's.
- Keep the fire small and controlled at all times.
- Have water and sand nearby in case you need to put out the fire.

How to make

1 Gather your materials from the area around you. Only choose items that have already fallen to the ground. Never take them off a living tree.

2 Your campsite should have a designated area for the fire. Clear the space of any leaves, twigs and debris.

3 Lay down a bundle of tinder in the centre of the firepit.

4 Use your kindling to build a teepee shape above the tinder.

5 Ask an adult to light the tinder.

6 As the fire grows and burns, ask an adult to continue adding large pieces of kindling and logs as fuel.

When you're done with your fire, let it burn out. Ask an adult to pour water over it to ensure all the embers are out (nothing is still glowing).

See pages 122–123 for some top marshmallow-toasting tips!

 **CAMPERS 1+** (PLUS ONE ADULT)

HARNESS THE SUN

When you're outside, use what the **great outdoors** has to offer! Make your very own **solar-powered oven** to harness the **power of the sun** and bake **delicious** treats.

You will need
- Empty takeaway pizza box or slim cardboard box
- Scissors
- Aluminium foil
- Tape
- Thin black card or black duct tape
- Cling film
- Sticky tack
- Paper straw or pencil
- Sunny day

How to make

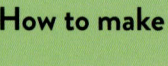

Stick foil under the flap.

Stick foil on the box base.

1 Ask an adult to cut a flap in the top of the pizza box. Fold it up along the top edge.

2 Cut a piece of foil the same size as the flap. Tape along the edges to secure it to the underside of the flap.

3 Open the box. Cut another piece of foil the same size as the box base. Tape it down inside the box, to line the bottom.

You could use black duct tape instead of black card.

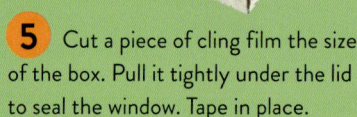
Tape cling film under the lid.

4 Cut a large square of thin black card. Tape it on the bottom layer of foil. This is your oven plate.

5 Cut a piece of cling film the size of the box. Pull it tightly under the lid to seal the window. Tape in place.

6 Place food on the black plate. You could use tortilla chips and grated cheese, or one of the suggestions on the page opposite. Close the lid.

DIPPING CHOCOLATE

Break a bar of chocolate into chunks and place it in a shallow bowl. Rest the bowl on the black plate. Once the chocolate has melted, dip fruit into it. Yum!

S'MORES

Place a digestive biscuit on the black plate. Put a marshmallow sandwiched in chocolate squares on top. Leave to melt!

Note: You can also make s'mores over the campfire. Flip to page 123 to find out how!

WARNING! Be careful when opening the oven. It can get hot inside. Place food out of reach of any animals.

7 Lift the flap and use sticky tack and the straw or pencil to prop it open.

8 Place your oven in a sunny spot outside, positioning the oven and flap so that the sun reflects off the flap and down on to the food below.

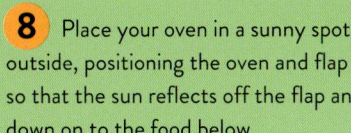

WHEN THE CHEESE HAS MELTED, OPEN THE LID AND ENJOY!

MORSE-CODE MESSAGES

Morse code can be a **life-saving skill**, as it can be used if you need to call for help. It can also be fun for sharing **secret messages** with your friends and family! **Learn the language**, then see if you can decode each other's sentences.

SECRET LANGUAGE

Morse code uses a series of dots and dashes to spell out letters and numbers.

A dot takes up one unit of space. A dash takes up three.

	F ··−·	M −−	T −
	G −−·	N −·	U ··−
A ·−	H ····	O −−−	V ···−
B −···	I ··	P ·−−·	W ·−−
C −·−·	J ·−−−	Q −−·−	X −··−
D −··	K −·−	R ·−·	Y −·−−
E ·	L ·−··	S ···	Z −−··

SECRET MESSAGES

How to make and play

You will need
- Short sticks and twigs
- Stones or pinecones

1 Decide on a short message you'd like to write, such as MEET AT THE TREE.

2 Look at the chart on the previous page to learn the sequence for each letter. Write out one letter at a time on the ground using your sticks as dashes and stones as dots. For example, M would be stick stick.

3 Continue step 2 until you've written your full message.

4 Ask a friend to decode the message using the chart. Then have them write a message for you to decipher!

Leave seven spaces between words and three spaces between letters.

TOP-SECRET TALK

You can also send Morse-code messages by tapping on a hard surface such as a table. A dot lasts for one time unit. A dash lasts for three time units. What else could you use from the campsite to send your messages? Try sending dots and dashes with short and long flashes of a torch in the dark. Ask a friend to stand a short distance away to watch the flashes carefully. Can they crack the code?

CAMPERS 1+

LOTS OF KNOTS

Don't tie yourself up in **knots**! Learn some different ways to knot rope and try them **for yourself**.

You will need
- Rope or cord

Reef knot
This basic knot is useful for tying together objects, such as a bundle of firewood or pieces of rope.

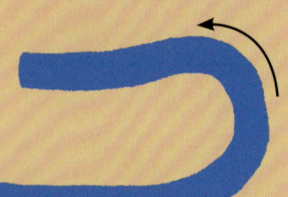

1 Curve one end of the rope.

2 Thread the other end of the rope through this curve towards you, then wrap it up behind the first section of rope.

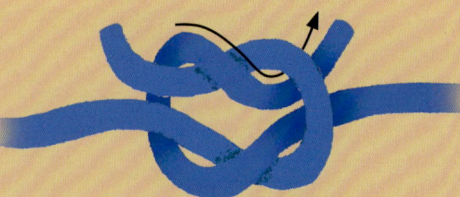

3 Thread the rope back through the loop.

4 Pull both ends to tighten.

Clove hitch
Use this knot to secure objects in place, such as the corners of tents to posts and pegs.

 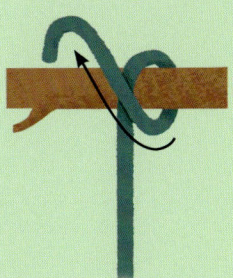 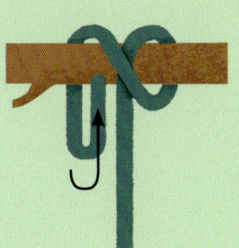 

1 Wrap one end of the rope around a pole or tree.

2 Loop the other end around the pole again, crossing over the first end of rope and behind the pole or tree.

3 Bring this end through the top loop.

4 Pull both ends to tighten.

Slip knot
The slip knot is a great multipurpose knot. You can use it to hang up items such as torches and lanterns, or to create loops for securing objects. It is easy to tighten with one end and loosen with the other.

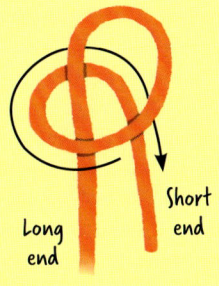 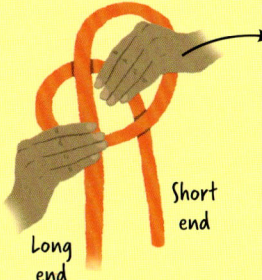 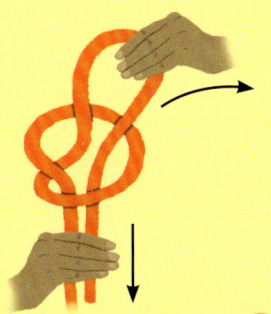 

1 Hold the rope about 20 cm (8 in) from the top and let it drop down. Form a loop by crossing the short end of the rope in front of the long end and then passing it around behind.

2 Holding the loop in place with one hand, use your other hand to reach through the loop and grab a section of the rope from the short end.

3 With one hand, pull the loop up. With the other hand, pull the two ends of the rope down. This will tighten your knot and leave a loop at the top.

4 To untie the knot, simply pull the short end downwards.

That's KNOT the end!
There are many more types of knots. Does your guidebook have others that you can try? Test out different knots for securing different items. Which do you find works best?

CAMPERS 1+

SUNNY TIMES

You will need
- Sunny day
- Clear area
- 2 sticks
- About 12 stones
- Felt-tip pen
- Watch

Go old school and **tell the time** by the position of the **sun in the sky**. You'll need a **sunny day** and a **clear space** to get started.

How to make

1 Start at the beginning of the day. Choose a clear, flat space that is not blocked by trees' shadows. Clear the area of any leaves, twigs and debris.

2 Push one stick straight into the ground.

3 Use your other stick to draw a circle in the dirt around the standing stick.

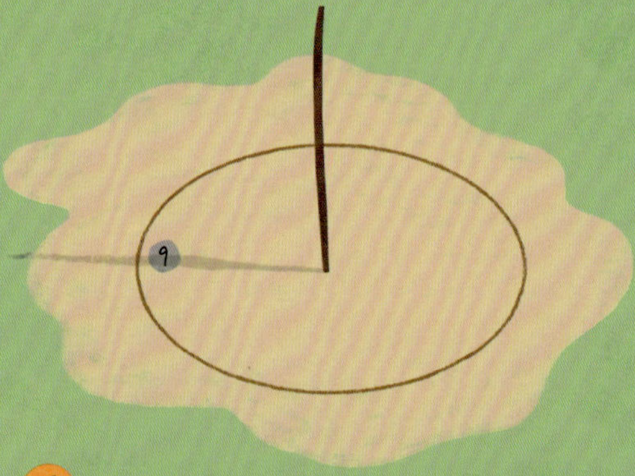

4 At 9am, check where the stick's shadow touches the circle. Label one stone with a number 9 and place it inside the circle at the point where the shadow falls.

5 Repeat step 4 every hour, with a new number to match the current time, until the sun disappears and you have lots of stones spaced out along the inside of the circle.

IT'S 3PM!

How to use
Leave the sundial in place for the next few days. If it's a sunny day, you can use the sundial to tell the time! Look where the stick's shadow falls on your circle. If it is touching a stone, you know the hour of day. If it is past a stone, you can estimate a quarter past, half past or quarter to the next stone. Check against a watch. Did your sundial tell the correct time?

CAMPSITE GAMES

Look around you... everything can be turned into a **game or playing piece** if your creative juices are flowing! Use sticks, pinecones, camping tables and even empty jars to have fun around the campground. Gather a few players, and **let the games begin**!

CAMPERS 2+

HUNT FOR TREASURE

You will need
- Paper
- Pens
- Something to hide as treasure, such as a toy, or food in a sealed snack pot
- Black card
- Scissors
- Tape or glue
- White pencil

Step up your map skills by placing **treasure** at the end of a trail. **Play pirates** and hide loot for each other to find. **X marks the spot!**

Draw your tent as the starting point.

START

Draw a trail with a dashed line for the treasure-hunters to follow.

Picnic area

Stony bridge

Washing-up area

Hidden treasure
Think about where you could hide your treasure on the campground. Could you perch a teddy in a tree? Dig a hole for a sealed pot of snacks? If you have a box and felt-tip pens, you could decorate it to look like a treasure chest.

Sand pit

Boulders

Play area

Lake

Stream

Map it up
Instead of drawing a map, you could use a real map of the campground. Ask an adult to hide treasure nearby and mark the spot on the map with an X. Then use your map-reading and compass skills (see page 21) to find the treasure.

Add landmarks for them to look out for to guide them along the way.

Woods

Tree swing

Campsite shop

FINISH

Pirate play
Make pirate hats out of card to really get into character. Draw the shape of the hat on a piece of black card. Cut this out. Draw a skull and crossbones in the centre. Trace this piece onto another piece of black card. Cut it out. Place the two pieces on top of each other, skull and crossbones facing out. Tape or glue the ends of the two pieces together. Open up the middle section. Place this on your head!

This should be three times the width of your head.

CAMPERS 2+

OBSTACLE COURSE

Create an **obstacle course** using items from around the campground. Set it up, then try it out yourself. **Challenge** a friend or family member too!

You will need
- Outdoor chalk (optional)
- Rope, string or skipping rope
- Paper cups
- Ball
- Sticks
- Flat piece of wood
- Logs
- Buckets
- Pinecones
- Stones

Hopscotch
Draw a hopscotch grid in the dirt with a stick, or on a pavement with chalk. Hop, skip and jump your way across. You could add an item such as a small stone to collect along the way.

Limbo lane
Tie rope or string around two trees to create a straight line about chest height. Lean back as you walk to pass under it. Move the rope further down to increase the difficulty.

Cup dodge
Set out camping cups (or large stones or buckets) in a line. Dribble a ball through the cups, weaving around each one as you go. You could also try weaving around trees on your campsite!

Stick hop
Lay out a series of sticks horizontally, leaving enough space in between for a person to stand. Start at one end and hop over each stick one at a time to get to the other side.

Balance beam
Lay a rope along the ground. Can you balance to walk along it? Step up the difficulty with a flat piece of wood laid across two logs. Just have an adult nearby in case things get wobbly!

Pinecone toss
Set up buckets a few paces away. Lay rope down or draw a line in the dirt with a stick. Stand behind the line and toss pinecones, small stones or balls into the buckets. Can you get one in each bucket? Place the buckets at different distances to make some harder than others.

Put it all together!
Set a start and finish for your obstacle course. How quickly can you complete all the challenges? You could time each person as they go through.

CAMPERS 2+

WATER GAMES

You will need
- Water (from a tap or nearby water source)
- Buckets or big bowls
- Sponges
- Cups
- Sticks

On a warm and sunny day, get the **water out to play**! Gather a few players – the more the better. Try to stay dry, but be prepared to **get wet**!

FILL IT UP

How to play

1 If there are at least four players, divide into two teams. For a smaller number of players, play individually.

2 Set up one bucket full of water per team or individual. Place these in a line.

3 About 2 m (6.5 feet) away, place empty buckets in line with the full ones.

4 On 'Go', one player from each team soaks a sponge with water in the full bucket. They then run to the empty bucket and wring out as much water as they can into it.

5 Continue with step 4, taking it in turns if there is more than one player on a team. When the first bucket is empty, the team with the highest filled bucket wins!

If you don't have a bucket and sponge, use a washing-up bowl and tea towel.

PASS IT ON

How to play

1 Stand in a line, with everyone facing the back of the person in front of them.

2 Each person holds a camping cup or small bucket, such as a sand bucket. The person at the front of the line has their cup or bucket full of water. Everyone else has an empty cup or bucket.

3 Without turning around, the person at the front of the line lifts the cup over their head and very carefully pours the water backwards into the cup of the person behind. This person can move their cup around to try to catch as much water as possible. The person at the front then runs to the back of the line.

4 Repeat step 3 until all the water is gone. How long can you make it last?

For an extra challenge, try holding the cup of water above your head!

WATER CHALLENGE

Set up a series of cups and sticks. Weave your way through the cups and step over the sticks – all while carrying a very full cup of water. Who can reach the end with the most water still in their cup?

CAMPERS 2+

SPORTS DAY

It's sports day, camping edition! Get in the spirit with a full **day of events**. Who will come out **on top**?

Pinecones on spoons
You're unlikely to have spare eggs for racing, but don't let that stop you! Grab pinecones or small stones from the ground around you. Each person needs a large spoon too. Set a starting line and a finish line. Everyone stands at the starting line balancing their pinecone on their spoon. Holding the spoon out in front of them, players must race to the finish line without letting the pinecone fall. The first person to cross the line with the pinecone on the spoon wins! If the pinecone falls off the spoon as you go, stop to place it back on the spoon before moving again.

Sleeping bag races
Try this camping twist on the classic sack race. Choose a starting line, and a finish line 10 paces away. Each person stands in a sleeping bag at the starting line. On 'Go', jump in your sleeping bags all the way to the finish. Hold on tight! The first person to cross the line wins.

Be sure no people or tents are in the way!

Make medals
For each event, you could award first, second and third place. Trace or draw circles onto card. Write 1st, 2nd or 3rd on each one. Cut out the circles and attach string to place the medals around the winners' necks.

Welly throw
Find a clear, open space. Scrape a starting line in the ground or place a rope or long stick across the grass. Everyone must be positioned behind this line. Take it in turns to toss a welly (or shoe) as far as you can from the line. After each throw, mark where the welly landed with a stone. You could use a felt-tip pen to label the stones with each person's name or initials. After everyone has had a go, see whose stone is the farthest from the starting line. That person is the winner!

Invent your own
Look at the space and materials around your campsite. What other sporting events could you hold? Try a classic sprint race if you've got room. Or divide into teams and challenge each other to a tug of war if you've got some spare strong rope. What about racing with a sock balanced on your head instead of a beanbag?

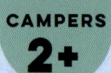

CAMPERS 2+

CREEPY-CRAWLY BINGO

Look high and low and **pay close attention** to the wildlife around you to come out on top in this game that's **crawling** with fun. Make your own playing boards, then see who can be the first to shout '**Bingo!**'.

You will need
- Paper
- Ruler
- Pencil
- Felt-tip pens

How to make

1 Use your ruler and pencil to draw six vertical lines and six horizontal lines on a sheet of paper, to create a 5 x 5 grid of 25 squares.

2 In the centre square, draw a star. This is a free space that counts as one of your completed squares.

3 In the other 24 squares, write the names of different insects, bugs and other critters that you might spot around the campground.

4 Repeat steps 1 to 3 to create a bingo board for each person playing. Write the items in different spaces on the board so that no boards are the same. You could also include different items on each board to make it interesting!

How to play

Throughout your camping holiday, keep your eyes peeled for the creatures on your board. This might be around the campsite, on nature walks or as you go for a drive. Every time you spot one of the creatures, tick it off your board with a felt-tip pen. The goal is to complete a line of five (across, down or diagonally). As soon as you do, shout out 'Bingo!'. The first person to shout 'Bingo!' wins.

Beetle	Centipede	Fly	Spider	Bumblebee
Wasp	Butterfly	Worm	Ladybird	Grasshopper
Slug	Firefly	FREE SPACE	Ant	Dragonfly
Moth	Frog	Caterpillar	Stick insect	Mosquito
Pigeon	Snail	Blackbird	Squirrel	Dung beetle

Go beyond bugs to fill your board! What else might you spot?

Bird bingo

Instead of creepy-crawlies, use a guidebook to fill your grid with all sorts of different birds that you might spot on your camping holiday. Look carefully to identify them in the wild (but don't touch!).

CAMPERS 2+

SUPER SPOTTER

Keep your eyes peeled to **rack up the points** in this game of spotting around the campground. Make a list of items you might see, assign points to each one and then **get spotting**!

You will need
- Paper
- Felt-tip pens or pencils

How to make and play

1 On the paper, write or draw a list of things that you might see around the campground.

2 Assign each item a points value from 1 to 5. Things that are common to spot, such as a tree, might be worth 1 point. Things that are rare, such as an owl, could be worth the full 5.

3 On another piece of paper, draw a tally chart with a column for each person playing. Write the name of each player at the top of each column.

4 Each time someone is the first to spot one of the items on your list, write the item and its points value in the spotter's column on the tally chart.

5 At the end of your camping holiday, add up the points in each column. The person with the highest value wins!

CAMPERS 2+

TOWER CHALLENGE

You will need
- Sticks
- Timer
- Marshmallows (optional)

Test your building skills in this **sky-high** challenge. Who can build **the tallest tower** – before it comes toppling down?

How to play

1 Gather as many sticks as you can.

2 Set a timer for 2 minutes. When the timer starts, each player begins building a tower. Build it as high as you can, but keep it steady too.

3 When the timer ends, see whose tower is tallest – and whose is still standing!

TICK TOCK

Include a time limit for a shorter time if you want to make this challenge harder. Give players longer (or no time limit at all) for an easier version.

What's your technique?

There are many different ways to build towers. Which will you try to reach the greatest heights?

Teepee

In a jumble

In a square

Carefully placing your sticks at right angles may help you to build a more solid tower.

Sticky marshmallows could hold the sticks together.

Engineered

Team building
Instead of competing, work as a team to gather larger sticks and branches, then make a big tower together. How high can you build it before it falls down?

CAMPERS 2

TABLE TENNIS

Take to the table and get that ball **ping-ponging** back and forth. Use materials around you to make paddles and a net, then turn a camping table into a court. **Game on!**

You will need
- Thick cardboard, such as from a pizza box
- Pencil
- Scissors
- 4 ice lolly sticks
- Glue
- Tape
- Sticks
- Rope or string
- Small, light ball, such as a ping-pong ball
- Folding camping table

How to make

1 Draw a large paddle shape (like a round tree with a trunk, as shown) on the thick cardboard. Cut it out.

2 Trace this shape on another piece of cardboard and cut out.

3 Lay two ice lolly sticks on the long end of one paddle shape. Glue in place.

4 Glue the second paddle shape on top of the first, sandwiching the sticks in the middle. Press down and leave to dry.

5 Wrap tape around the handle to strengthen it.

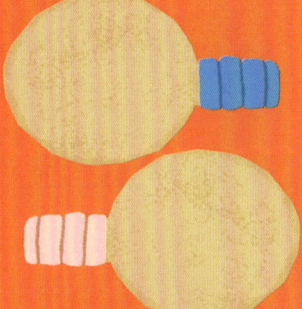

6 Repeat steps 1 to 5 to make a second paddle.

Use what you've got
If you haven't got the materials to make paddles, try holding a plastic plate to bat the ball, or a thick stick (carefully!). For the net, lay a piece of string across the table to mark the middle. For the ball, you could use scrunched-up paper.

For the net, tape a stick to each side of the centre of your table. Wind rope back and forth a few times between the sticks. Tie with a knot to secure.

How to play

1 Each player stands at either end of the table holding their paddle.

2 Player 1 uses the paddle to bounce the ball on their side of the table and over the net. This is called serving.

3 The player on the other side (player 2) should let the ball bounce once on their side of the table. They then try to hit the ball back towards player 1. If player 2 cannot return the ball, player 1 earns a point.

4 Play continues back and forth. Each time a player cannot return the ball, the other player wins a point. When the ball falls, take it in turns to serve it again.

5 The first player to earn 11 points wins!

Or, you could simply try to rally the ball back and forth over the net. How many times can you hit it before it falls?

CAMPERS 4+ (PLUS ONE ADULT)

BALL GAMES

The simple ball can give you **countless games** to play! Pick up a beach ball, tennis ball, football, basketball or any other ball you can find and try these ideas to **get the ball rolling**.

SIMON SAYS

Choose one person to be Simon. Simon stands facing everyone else in the group. Everyone must be holding a ball. Simon then gives instructions of things to do with the ball. If Simon starts the instruction with 'Simon says...' then everyone must do what Simon says. But if Simon doesn't say 'Simon says...' first, ignore the instruction! Anyone who does it anyway is out. Who will be the last person standing?

SIMON SAYS TOSS THE BALL.

SIMON SAYS LIE DOWN NEXT TO THE BALL.

SIMON SAYS SIT ON THE BALL!

HOLD THE BALL ABOVE YOUR HEAD.

YOU'RE OUT!

CATCH OR NOT

Stand in a circle. Choose one person to stand in the centre with a ball. They throw the ball to someone in the circle, saying 'Catch!' or 'Don't catch!' The person in the circle must think fast to follow the instruction. If they do the opposite of what the thrower said, they're out. The person in the centre continues going around the circle, throwing to each person one at a time with the instruction. The last person left in the circle wins!

To make the game even trickier, each player does the opposite of the thrower's command. So if the thrower says 'Don't catch!' the player actually tries to catch the ball!

HOT POTATO

Sit in a circle. One person holds a ball. Ask an adult to be in charge of the music. When the music starts, the person holding the ball passes it to their left. Everyone must continue passing on the ball as quickly as they can – pretend it's a very hot potato! When the music stops, the person holding the ball is out (or, they can stay in and just try again). Try this game standing, sitting and even passing the ball with your feet instead of your hands!

And more!
What else can you do with just a ball? How about...
- Count how many times you can toss it back and forth with a friend without dropping it.
- Count how many times you can bounce it on the ground with your hand.
- Count how many times you can bounce it on your knee WITHOUT using your hands. Keep trying to beat your best scores!

CAMPERS 2+

FAIRGROUND FUN

Step right up! Save materials such as empty cans, glass jars and toilet rolls to create your own games, and **bring the funfair** to your campground.

RING TOSS

You will need
- 5 sticks
- 5 empty toilet rolls or kitchen roll tubes
- Felt-tip pen
- 5 paper plates
- Scissors
- String

How to make and play

1 Push one stick straight into the ground.

2 Push the other four sticks into the ground around this one, as shown below.

3 Write the numbers 5, 10, 15, 20 and 25 on the cardboard rolls. These are the points values.

4 Place the tube labelled 25 over the stick in the middle. Place the 5 tube on the stick closest to you, and the other three tubes on the remaining three sticks.

5 Carefully cut the centre out of each paper plate so that you're left with just the outer ring.

6 Make a line on the ground with string or a stick. Stand behind this line to play. From here, toss each ring, one at a time. Try to get each ring to land on one of the tubes. Once you have tossed all five paper plates, add up your points!

COIN DROP

You will need
- Bucket
- Small glass jar
- Water
- Coins

How to make and play

  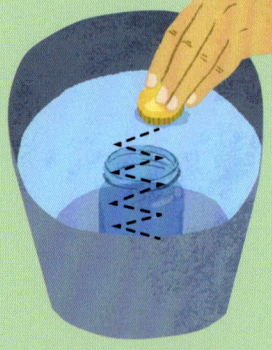

1 Fill a bucket about two-thirds full of water.

2 Place the glass jar at the bottom of the bucket. Put a few coins in it to weigh it down.

3 To play, hold a coin flat on the surface of the water, then let go! Who can get their coin to land in the jar? It's harder than it sounds!

TIN CAN TUMBLE

You will need
- 6 clean, empty cans (be careful that the edges aren't sharp)
- String
- Ball

How to make and play

1 Build a tall triangle shape out of your tin cans.

2 Make a line on the ground with string. Stand behind this line to play. From here, a player can throw the ball three times to try to knock down the tower.

Fun at the fair
For a full fairground experience, you could cut up paper into small tokens. Players can use these tokens to 'pay' to play the games. You could even have prizes to win, such as seashells, or a treat from the snack bag.

CAMPING CRAFTS

Get crafty in the **great outdoors**! Discover a-MAZE-ing sticks, unbe-LEAF-able leaves, stones that ROCK and many more incredible art supplies hiding in your natural surroundings. Gather your materials, **get creative** and let your **artistic side loose**!

CAMPERS 1+

MAKE A NATURE COLLAGE

Note: Never take items off living trees or plants. There should be plenty to discover on the ground at your feet!

Anything can be turned into art if you **look closely**. Gather natural items from around you and piece them together into a **beautiful picture** to remember your time at the campsite.

You will need
- Items from around the campsite, such as twigs, leaves, pinecones, moss and flower petals
- Paper
- Glue
- Felt-tip pens (optional)

Think about how different natural pieces can fit into your art.

Lay out your items as a picture on your paper. This might be an abstract collection, or you could use your items to create a picture, such as a butterfly or tree.

CAMPERS 1+ (PLUS ONE ADULT)

PAINT WITH NATURE

You will need
- Paint
- Paper plate
- Items from around the campsite, such as twigs, sticks, clean feathers, leaves, pinecones, moss, small stones and flowers
- Paper
- Baking tray, chopping board or other flat surface

When in nature, use what you've got **around you**. Twigs can become paintbrushes, pinecones can become stamps and berries can turn into paint! What else can you **create**?

PAINTBRUSHES

Squeeze out paint onto a paper plate. Try dipping different natural items, such as sticks, clean feathers and flowers, into the paint. Use these to paint on your paper. Which do you like working with best?

ON A ROLL

Place a piece of paper onto a baking tray or other flat surface. Dip small stones into paint so that they're completely covered. Place a stone at one end of the paper. Holding the paper and baking tray carefully at each end, tip the tray so that the stone rolls down. Continue tipping the tray at different angles to create a pattern. Try dipping different stones in different paint colours to create a multicoloured picture!

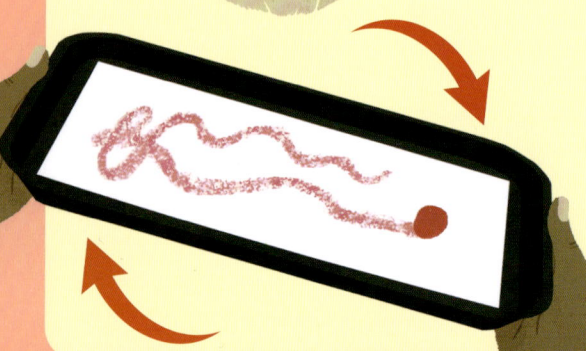

STAMPS

Items with a flat or interesting surface work well as stamps. Try dipping the end of a stick into paint and then stamping it onto your paper. What pattern appears? Ask an adult to cut a small apple in half. Dip this into your paint and stamp it onto paper. What do you see now? What other materials work as stamps? You could try the side of a pinecone, a handful of moss, a seashell, flower heads or a leaf too.

MAKE YOUR OWN PAINT

Ask an adult to help you make your very own paint! Different plants will give you different colours. For example, you can create red paint from cranberries and strawberries and purple paint from blueberries, blackberries and blackcurrants.

You will need
- Berries (check with an adult that they're safe to pick and use)
- Sieve
- Bowl
- Water
- Spoon
- Paintbrush
- Paper

1 Gather safe berries from around your campground.

2 Press the berries through a sieve. Collect the juices in a bowl.

3 Add just a dash of water and stir with a spoon. The mixture should be thick enough to paint with and not so runny that it spreads across your page.

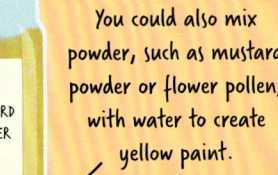

You could also mix powder, such as mustard powder or flower pollen, with water to create yellow paint.

Note: Wear old clothes or an apron, as natural paints can stain.

CAMPERS 1+ (PLUS ONE ADULT)

CAMPSITE CROWNS

Use natural items to make a **decorative crown**, then declare yourself **king or queen of the camp!**

You will need
- Cardboard
- Scissors
- Tape
- Items from around the campsite, such as bark, pinecones, leaves and flowers
- Glue
- Paint and paintbrush (optional)

Small flowers could be used to look like jewels.

Tape two pieces of cardboard together if your first piece isn't long enough.

What's your style?

Will you go for a royal design to rule the campsite, or will you choose a more playful woodland elf crown? Will you place pieces of bark or sticks next to each other all the way around your crown, or go for a more dotted design? You decide! You could even try making other campground accessories. What about a simple flower bracelet or chunky pinecone belt?

Try these designs.

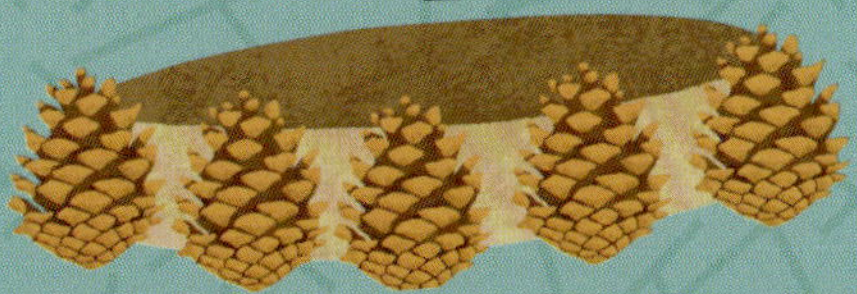

Pinecone belt

Bark crown

You could paint the cardboard before you use it, or leave it natural!

How to make

1 Cut a long thick strip of cardboard.

2 Ask an adult to help you wrap the strip around your head. Tape the ends together. Remove the crown from your head and cut off any excess.

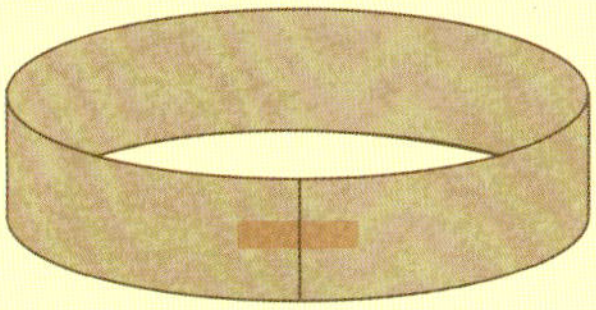

3 Glue your natural items onto the crown. Place long items, such as twigs, grass and leaves, vertically so they point up on the crown. Leave to dry.

CAMPERS 2+

STICK MAZES

Did you know even the plain stick can be **a-MAZE-ing**? Gather a pile of sticks and turn them into a maze for **others to follow**. Can they find their **way out**?

You will need
- Lots of big sticks of various lengths
- A clear, open space

Use a clear, open space on the ground. Lay the sticks down so people can walk between them in a human-sized maze!

Leave an open space as the starting point.

START

Use smaller sticks to block off paths and larger sticks for the long edges.

Carefully lay out your sticks in a maze shape. Be sure to create pathways, dead ends and a way out.

FINISH

Swap sides
Have someone else at the camp create a maze for you. Can you tiptoe through and find the path out?

FINISH

START

Mini maze
If you haven't got the space, or big enough sticks, downsize! Place small twigs on a piece of paper to create a maze that others can follow with their finger or pen. Snap the twigs into smaller pieces to create all the paths and corners.

You could leave treasure, such as stones or seashells, for people to collect along the way. Let them know how many items they must find in total before they set off.

63

CAMPERS 1+

LEAF RUBBINGS

You will need
- Leaves
- Paper
- Crayons

Discover **patterns and textures** by rubbing crayons across paper and leaves for some **unbe-LEAF-able** art.

How to make

Always take these from the ground and not off a living tree!

The veins are the lines you can see in the leaf. You should be able to feel them raised up on one side.

Note: If your crayons have a paper wrapping, remove it.

1 Collect leaves from around your campsite. Make sure they are intact and dry.

2 Lay a leaf on a hard flat surface, such as a table, with the veins facing up.

Ask an adult to help you hold your leaf and paper in place if needed.

3 Lay a piece of paper over the leaf. Hold your crayon flat and rub it on the paper across where the leaf lies underneath. You should see the pattern of the leaf appear.

4 Repeat steps 2 and 3 for other leaves, moving the paper around as needed.

Use different coloured crayons to build up a pattern of leaves on your paper.

Try different-shaped leaves from different types of trees. What designs can you create?

Beyond leaves
Once you've got the hang of rubbing leaves, try the same technique on other natural materials. Try taking rubbings of tree bark or flat stones. Which do you like the best?

You could find loose tree bark and follow the same steps. Or, place a piece of paper on a tree trunk and rub your crayon across to copy a pattern straight from nature!

CAMPERS 1+ (PLUS ONE ADULT)

BUBBLE FUN

Bubbles are sure to **bring fun to everyone** at camp, both young and old. Use materials from around the campsite to have a **bubble-tastic time**.

MAKE YOUR OWN BUBBLE SOLUTION

You will need
- 6 tablespoons of washing-up liquid
- 2 cups of water
- Bowl
- Spoon

How to make

Gently stir the washing-up liquid and water together in the bowl. Make more solution as required.

BUBBLE SNAKE

You will need
- Recycled plastic bottle (empty and cleaned out)
- Scissors
- Sock or cloth
- Elastic band
- Bubble solution (see above)

How to make and play

1 Ask an adult to carefully cut the bottom end off the plastic bottle.

2 Wrap the sock or cloth over the cut end of the bottle. Use an elastic band to secure in place.

3 Dip the fabric end of the bottle into your homemade bubble solution. Blow through the drinking end of the bottle and watch a bubble snake appear!

How long can you make your bubble snake?

WARNING! Always blow out, never suck in, so you don't get a mouthful of bubbles.

BUBBLE WAND

How to make and play

1. Hold the two pieces of string together, lining up one end of each. Tie these ends together around the top of one stick.

2. Grab the loose ends of each piece of string and line these up. Tie these together around the top of the other stick.

3. Hold the sticks close to the bottom ends. Dip the string into your bubble solution. Carefully lift out the wand so that bubble mixture shows in the loop of string.

4. Gently blow through the loop to make bubbles!

You will need
- 30 cm (12 in) piece of string
- 50 cm (20 in) piece of string
- 2 sticks
- Bubble solution (see opposite page)

Can you see a rainbow in the bubbles as they catch the light?

CAMPERS 1+ (PLUS ONE ADULT)

MAKE YOUR OWN BINOCULARS

Binoculars help you focus on wildlife that you want to see clearly. Make your **very own pair** and see what you can spot!

You will need
- 2 toilet roll tubes (or 1 kitchen roll tube cut in half)
- Felt-tip pens
- Pencil
- Glue
- String

How to make

You could wrap string or an elastic band around the two tubes to help them stay together.

1 Colour and decorate the tubes using your felt-tip pens. Ask an adult to use a sharp pencil to poke a hole in each tube, about a third of the way down.

2 Place the two tubes next to each other, holes facing outwards. Glue the tubes together in the middle. Press together gently to help them stick.

3 Thread the string through one tube. Tie a couple of knots in the end of the string inside the tube so that it can't be pulled through.

Be ready!
Wear the binoculars around your neck to keep them handy. If you hear a little chirp, lift them up and peer through.

4 Loop the string around and thread it through the other hole. Check that it is the right length to get over your head, then tie a knot inside the second tube so that the string stays in place. Cut off any excess.

CAMPERS 1+ (PLUS ONE ADULT)

WILD WINDSOCK

Check the direction and the strength of the wind with a **homemade windsock**. Hang it in an open space and **watch the wind blow!**

You will need
- Toilet or kitchen roll tube
- Colouring pencils or paint
- Scissors
- String
- Long grass and/or clean feathers
- Tape

Decorate a toilet roll with your paint or pencils.

Ask an adult to poke a hole on each side of the top of the toilet roll. Thread a long piece of string through both holes to make a handle. Tie each end in place.

Tape long pieces of grass around the inside of the bottom edge of the toilet roll. Let them hang down from the roll.

Ask an adult to poke small holes around the bottom of the toilet roll. Tie short pieces of string to the ends of clean feathers. Tie the other ends of the string through the holes in the roll. Let the feathers hang down.

Note: Always wash your hands after handling feathers.

Ways of the windsock
Hang your windsock in a high, clear place so the feathers and grass will catch the breeze. Which way is the wind blowing today?

Remember to take your windsock away when you leave. Take it inside when it's raining too.

CAMPERS 1+ (PLUS ONE ADULT)

FLYING HIGH

You will need
- 2 sticks, one slightly longer than the other
- Ball of string
- Scissors
- Old plastic carrier bag
- Permanent pen
- Tape

Let's go **fly a kite**! Reuse a carrier bag to make your very own kite. Then wait for a breezy day and **let it fly**! Be patient and you should **see it soar**.

How to make

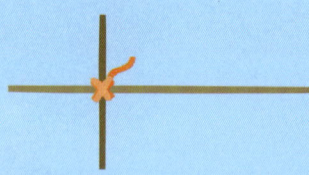
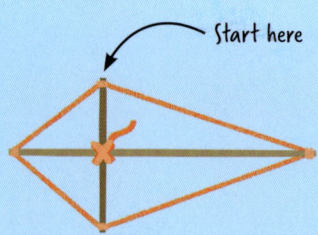

Start here

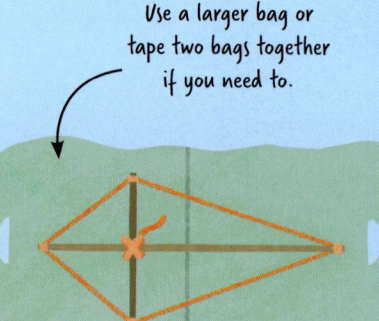

Use a larger bag or tape two bags together if you need to.

1 Lay the short stick on top of the long stick as shown. Wrap string in a figure-of-eight motion around the join several times to attach the sticks together. Tie a knot and cut off any excess string.

2 Tie string around one end of the frame as shown. Pull it tightly to one end of the long stick. Tie another knot. Continue pulling tight and knotting at each end of the frame until you return to the point where you began. You should have a diamond shape.

3 Cut down the two edges of the carrier bag and open it out so you have a flat sheet. Lay the kite frame on top of the bag.

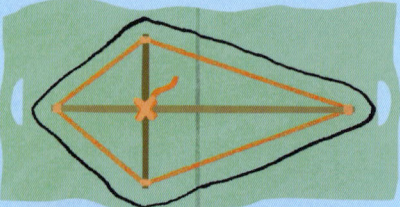
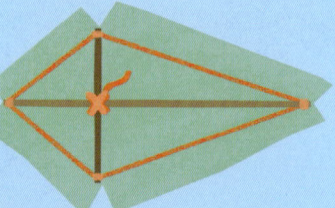
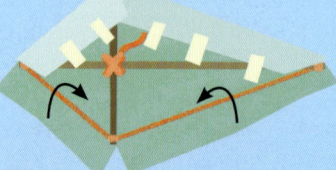

4 Draw around the kite frame with a permanent pen, marking the plastic about 2.5 cm (1 in) away from the frame edges. Cut out.

5 Cut a 2.5 cm (1 in) notch into each corner.

6 Working on one edge at a time, fold the excess plastic over the string of the frame. Use tape to secure. Once you have completed all four edges, you will have a kite sail.

7 Measure and cut a piece of string as long as the long stick plus 15 cm (6 in). Tie the ends of the string to either end of the long stick.

8 Measure and cut a piece of string to attach to each end of the short stick, meeting the long string in the middle. Tie the ends of the string to either end of the short stick.

Kite-flying tips

- Find a clear, open space so your kite won't get caught on any trees.

- Wait for a breeze. You need a wind strong enough to catch the sail, but not so strong that it batters your kite!

- To get started, ask an adult to hold up your kite a few paces away, while you hold onto the ball of string. When the breeze comes, ask your adult to let go.

- Keep the line of string fairly short to begin with. Once your kite catches the wind, slowly let more string out so the kite can fly higher.

- Add more tails to your kite if you need more weight.

- Tighten the knots and secure any loose ends with tape as you go to keep your kite in tip-top flying shape.

- Be patient! Sometimes it can take a while for a kite to catch the breeze.

9 Tie the end of your ball of string to the point where the two pieces of string cross.

10 Cut strips from the remaining plastic of your carrier bag. Tape one strip to the bottom point of the sail to create a tail. Tie other pieces to this tail to make the tail longer.

Now test your kite!

WARNING! Never fly your kite near overhead cables.

Note: Be sure to take your kite home with you and not leave any plastic in nature.

CAMPERS 1+

WALKING STICK

You're sure to do lots of **nature walks** on your camping holiday. Create your very own **personalised walking stick** to help you along the way.

You will need
- Long stick
- String
- Scissors
- Natural items from around the campsite, such as long grass, flowers, clean feathers and leaves

How to make

1 Choose a long stick to be your walking stick.

Knot

2 Knot the string around one end of the stick. Wrap it around and around, all the way up to the other end of the stick.

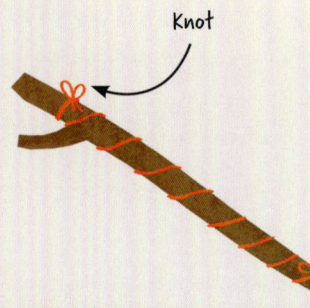

Knot

3 Tie a knot to secure the string to the stick. Cut off any excess.

Remember, this stick is all about you!

It's a walk in the park!

4 As you walk along, gather natural items from the ground. These could be things that you like the look of, or items that mean something to you, such as long grass from where you stopped for a picnic.

5 Tuck the items snugly between the string and stick. Continue adding items as you go until your stick is complete!

Top tip!
The best walking sticks are about as high as your waist or chest so that you can grip them naturally beside you. Choose a stick that feels solid and fairly straight too.

Every stick has a story
Around the campfire, or back home after your holiday, you could use this stick to tell stories of the adventures you had. Look at the items on the stick to share the story of your nature walk. Each item should help you remember where you were and what you did!

CAMPERS 1+

CRAFTS THAT ROCK

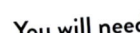

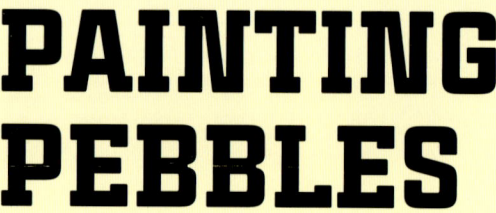

Use your imagination, and suddenly rocks can become so much more than simply a plain grey stone! Turn them into **works of art** and even pets.

PAINTING PEBBLES

Choose some smooth rocks and get crafty! Wash your rocks and let them dry in the sun. Then use paint or permanent markers to draw designs on them. You could choose rocks that look like certain creatures too, such as a pointy rock for a hedgehog or a round rock for a ladybird. What ROCKIN' looks will you create?

You will need
- Small rocks
- Paint and paintbrushes or permanent markers
- Glue (optional)

You might need more than one coat of paint if you're using light colours on a dark-coloured rock. Allow the paint to dry between coats.

Acrylic paint sticks to rocks best, but use what you've got!

Glue on smaller stones for eyes and noses.

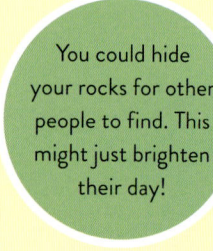

You could hide your rocks for other people to find. This might just brighten their day!

MY PET ROCK

Use materials around you to make your very own pet to have on holiday with you. And the best part is, there's no walking or cleaning up after them required!

You will need
- Rock
- Paint and permanent markers
- Empty, cleaned-out jar
- Natural items, such as grass, small twigs, leaves, sand or dirt, loose bark, etc.

Find a rock that's just the right size to be your pet. It should fit in the palm of your hand and inside the jar too.

Paint your rock, let it dry, then draw a face on it using your pens. Give it big eyes and a friendly smile — or whatever expression you'd like!

Create a home for your pet with a recycled jar.

Place natural items into the jar to make a cosy and comfy space for your rock.

You could layer materials inside your jar. Pour fine materials, such as sand and dirt, into the bottom. Place larger items, such as leaves, on top.

ROCKY'S HOME

Rock rules
Make sure the rocks are free to take. Some beaches and national parks don't want you taking their rocks away. Find loose rocks around your campsite and check with an adult that they're OK to use.

What will you name your rock? You could write the name on your jar.

THE GREAT OUTDOORS

When you're camping, the great outdoors itself can become your **playground and discovery centre**. **Switch on your senses**, and look, listen and get hands-on with your surroundings. Get to know trees, leaves, clouds and more as you search and record your discoveries. Grab your notebook and **go explore**!

CAMPERS 1+

GET TO KNOW TREES

The **great outdoors** is full of them – big and small, tall and short, leafy and prickly. But how well do you **really** know trees? Spend some time exploring and getting to know the **tree-rrific** space around you.

CLIMB A TREE

What better way to get to know a tree than by getting right in it? First, find the perfect climbing tree. Look for:
- A dry tree so it won't be slippery
- A tree with a thick trunk
- Solid, low branches for you to grab as you go

Check with an adult that your tree is safe. Then, get climbing!

Take your time and only go as high as you feel comfortable. Always think about how you'll get back down again. Keep three limbs (two hands and a foot or two feet and a hand) on the tree at all times. Settle in on a strong branch and enjoy the view!

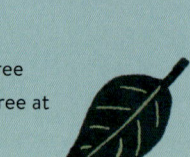

WORK OUT ITS AGE

Watch for a tree stump as you explore your surroundings. Then, look closely at the rings. If they're hard to see, you could wipe the top for a clearer view. Each ring of the tree represents one year of growth. Count the rings from the centre point all the way out to the bark. The number of rings is the age of your tree in years! So, if you count 20 rings, this means the tree was 20 years old when it fell.

LOOK AT LEAVES

There are thousands of species of trees across the world. Which ones can you find around your campsite? Look at the leaves you find to help you work out which tree is which. Use a guidebook to look up the leaves and match them to a type of tree. Try these to get started:

Beech · Elm · Willow · Acacia · Eucalyptus

Maple · Palm · Oak · Pine · Douglas fir

Some trees have needles instead of leaves.

Changing seasons
Deciduous trees shed their leaves every year, normally in autumn to grow new ones in the spring. If you're camping in autumn or winter, you might not find their leaves. Instead, you could look for **evergreen trees**. They stay green throughout the whole year.

Deciduous · Evergreen

CAMPERS 1+

NATURE JOURNAL

You will need
- 4 sheets of A4 paper
- 1 sheet of A4 card
- Hole punch (or a sharp tool, if an adult can help)
- Stick
- Elastic band
- Pens

There is so much to spot when you're out and about. **Make your own** nature journal to keep track of what you see. Decorate it in your own style, then **fill it with wonder**!

How to make

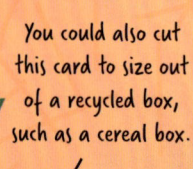

You could also cut this card to size out of a recycled box, such as a cereal box.

1 Place the 4 sheets of paper in a pile, long edge towards you. Make sure the edges are lined up, then fold the pile in half from left to right. Crease.

2 Fold the sheet of card in half in the same way. Wrap it over the stack of paper so the folds line up and you have a little covered booklet.

3 Carefully punch two holes in the pages, near to the fold edge.

If you don't have an elastic band, use string to tie the stick in place.

Wrap the band around twice if needed for it to stay in place.

4 Break your stick so that it's just long enough to cover both holes. Push one end of the elastic band up through the top hole from the back. Wrap it around the top end of the stick.

5 Push the other end of the elastic band up through the bottom hole from the back of the booklet. Wrap it around the bottom end of the stick. Pull tight.

6 Decorate the cover of your journal. You could add your name and natural drawings or patterns to make it your own. Now fill the journal with your discoveries!

CAMPERS 2+

SCAVENGER HUNT

Search high and low around your campsite as you race to complete this **nature scavenger hunt**. Who can tick all the items off their list?

You will need
- Paper
- Pens
- Bucket or basket (optional)
- Camera or smartphone (optional)

How to make and play

1 Each person taking part makes a list of 10 natural items on their piece of paper. These should be items that you can find around the campground.

2 Once everyone is done, swap pages so each person has a list that they didn't write.

3 Go seeking! The aim of the game is for each player to collect all 10 items on their list. You could set a time limit and see who collects the most items in that amount of time. Or, without a time limit, the first person to collect all 10 items wins!

WE'RE GOING ON A NATURE HUNT!

Instead of collecting the items, you could take a photo of them.

1. Pinecone
2. Stick ✓
3. Animal footprint (photo)
4. Leaf in the shape of a heart
5. Caterpillar (photo) ✓
6. Loose tree bark ✓
7. Feather
8. Clover
9. Rock
10. Flower

CAMPERS 1+ (PLUS ONE ADULT)

MAKE A MAGNIFYING GLASS

Look closer than ever before with this easy **homemade magnifying glass**. Reuse an empty plastic bottle, add a bit of water and hey presto! You can now **zoom in** on the **tiny world** around you.

How to make

> **WARNING!** Cut plastic can have sharp edges, so be extra careful.

You will need
- Empty, clean see-through plastic bottle
- Felt-tip pen
- Scissors
- Water

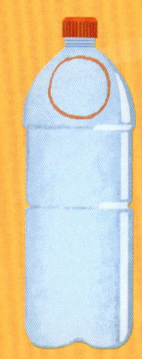

1 Draw a circle on the curved neck of the bottle.

2 Ask an adult to help you carefully cut out the circle. It will curve up into a shallow bowl-shaped disc once it's cut out.

3 Place the disc on a flat surface with its curved edges facing upwards. Add a few drops of water into the centre of the disc.

4 Hold the disc above an item that you want to see up close. You should notice that the item looks bigger through your magnifying glass!

CAMPERS 1+ (PLUS ONE ADULT)

NAME YOUR FINDS

There is so much information out there to help you become familiar with your surroundings and **get to know the nature** where you've set up camp. Find a field guide to help you identify and log your **discoveries**.

You will need
- Guidebook, field guide or online spotter sheets
- Paper or notebook

Step 1: Choose your guide
Find a guidebook or field guide that lists natural items that you might find in your local camping area. Will you look for rocks, plants or animals? Wildlife websites also often have free spotting sheets to download.

Step 2: Go explore
Head out into nature with your guide and an adult. Look closely around you to spot rocks, plants or animals. Compare what you find with the images in your field guide. Flip through until you find a match. Can you identify your discoveries by name?

Step 3: Log your findings
In your notebook, write down the name of the object or creature spotted, as well as the date, time and place.

Wildlife spotted			
Jelly ear fungus	June 20	4:50 pm	Sunnywood Campsite
Centipede	June 21	10:35 am	Treetop Trail
Poppy	June 21	10:40 am	Treetop Trail
Horse mushroom	June 23	9:00 am	Sunnywood Campsite

Top tip:
If you're spotting wildlife that moves, snap a quick pic! That way you can compare the image to your guide later if the creature flies or crawls away while you're flipping through the pages.

Picture perfect
Another way to track your finds is by location. Make a map of your campsite and the surrounding area. Draw interesting finds on the map, in the place where you spotted them.

CAMPERS 1+

CLOUD SPOTTING

Look up to the sky. What can you **spy**? The shapes and colours of clouds can tell you all about **the weather**. You can also find **fun shapes** in the clouds using your **own imagination**.

KNOW THE NAMES

There are 10 main types of clouds. Can you learn them all?

Look up at the sky at different points of your holiday, on rainy days and on clear days. Which types of clouds can you spot?

High clouds: Clouds high in the sky are thin and wispy. If you see them, there is very little chance of rain.

Cirrus   Cirrostratus   Cirrocumulus

Mid-level clouds: Clouds partway up the sky could mean that rain is on its way.

Altocumulus   Nimbostratus   Altostratus

Cumulonimbus clouds rise up from low to high. They are tall and stormy!

Low clouds: These puffy clouds are low to the ground.

Cumulus   Stratus   Stratocumulus

SEEING SHAPES

People like to see pictures in the strange shapes of clouds. On a clear day, find an open area. Lay down a picnic blanket and lie back on it, making sure you face away from the sun. Look up into the sky and let the clouds roll by. What can you see?

IT'S A DOG JUMPING!

I SEE A DRAGON!

A BROWN BEAR!

WARNING! Never look directly at the sun.

A RABBIT!

Carry on spotting
Slow down and spend time with the clouds.

- Record the different clouds you see in your nature journal. Draw pictures of them, write down what they looked like and when and where you saw them.

- Count all the clouds you can see in the sky.

- Play games with friends and family members. One person could name an object in the clouds, such as a dragon, and everyone else must point to which cloud they're talking about.

- Take a photo of interesting clouds using a smartphone. Then use the phone's editing tool to draw on details.

CAMPERS 1+ (PLUS ONE ADULT)

FEED THE BIRDS

Bring the birds to you with your very own bird feeder. Use a recycled carton and some materials from around your campsite to create a **feeding haven** for your **feathered friends**.

You will need
- Clean, empty drinks carton
- Scissors
- 2 thin sticks
- String
- Bird seed or your own homemade mix

How to make

1 Ask an adult to help you cut a window halfway up each side of the carton.

2 Ask an adult to make a hole under each window.

3 Poke a stick through the holes on two of the facing sides. Repeat for the other facing sides. You should now have a cross of sticks where small birds can perch.

Remember to take your bird feeder with you when you leave the campsite.

4 Ask an adult to make two holes in the top of the carton. Thread string through the holes and use this to hang your feeder from a tree branch. Tie a knot to hold in place. Fill the bottom of the feeder with bird seed.

CAMPERS 1+

BIRD SPOTTING

Which birds like to visit your campsite? Use a field guide to **get to know** the birds in your area. Can you learn them **by name** and recognise **their song**? Or, just spend some time watching them as they **fly by**!

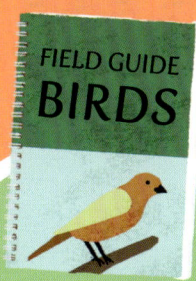

Find a field guide all about birds in your area. Compare the features of birds you spot with photos in the guide to identify the birds by name.

You will need
- Field guide
- Notebook and pen
- Binoculars (optional)
- Camera

See page 80 to make your own journal.

Keep a log of the birds you see. You could write down what they look like and draw a picture too. What shape are the wings, tail, feet and beak? What colour is the bird?

Listen! Birds have different calls. Can you identify the bird by the song it sings? Do you hear the same bird every day of your holiday?

Try making your own bird calls. Practise whistling. Find bird songs online that you can listen for and imitate.

Take photos of birds as you see them. This way you can still look them up after they fly away!

Top tips:
- If you hear a bird, stand still. The bird might just show itself to you!
- Look for birds early in the morning, when they are most active.
- Look all around you: up and down, in the sky and in the trees.
- Wear dark clothing so you blend into your surroundings.
- Never get too close to birds or their nests. Give them space!
- Be patient!

CAMPERS 1+

FINDING FOOTPRINTS

Step in **someone else's shoes** as you explore footprints on the ground below. Look down to find clues about the creatures that have **walked**, **hopped** or **crawled** the space before you. What can you **discover**?

You will need
- Magnifying glass (see how to make a small one on page 84)
- Notebook and pen
- Camera

Birds often have spiky footprints.

Sparrow

Swimming birds, such as ducks, have webbing too.

Use a local field guide to identify which creatures and tracks might be found near you.

Duck

Look in wet soil, where you'll find the best imprints and tracks.

Fox

CAMPERS 1+

BUG HOTEL

You will need
- Pieces of wood or logs
- Twigs and sticks
- Stones
- Dry leaves
- Dead grass
- Hay
- Bark

The great outdoors is home to loads of **creepy-crawly creatures**. Build them a **natural hideout** where they can choose to stay if they're looking for a place to shelter. Then open your **bug hotel**!

1 Select a spot
Choose a sheltered, shady spot that will stay cool for the critters. It's best to find a place next to a tree or bush.

2 Set up your structure
Using your wood and logs, build a structure with layers. Place larger logs at the bottom to keep the structure stable. Place a piece of wood across the top as a roof.

3 Fill the gaps
Fill the gaps between the layers with natural materials, such as sticks, stones, dry leaves and grass, hay and bark.

Pieces of bamboo or hollow stems provide tubes for bees to lay eggs.

Nooks, crannies and tunnels are perfect for insects to explore.

Place stones low down for frogs, newts and snails to keep cool.

Little insects such as ladybirds can hibernate in hay.

Note: Use natural items only so that you can leave the hotel in place when you leave the campsite.

Beetles and centipedes love to burrow in bark.

Anything goes
If you haven't got the materials to create a full hotel structure, make a log pile house instead. Gather some logs and pile them in a shady spot. Stuff material such as dry leaves and sticks into the gaps for insects to make themselves cosy.

CAMPERS 1+ (PLUS ONE ADULT)

CREATURES OF THE NIGHT

Some creatures are nocturnal – they are most active at **night**. When the sun has set and the stars are quietly shining, **listen closely**. What can you hear?

What to do
On a quiet night, sit still and close your eyes. Then listen carefully...

- Note down the sounds you hear in your journal. Listen over a few nights. Do you hear the same creatures over and over again? Can you make out anything new?

- Use a field guide to identify animals that might be in your area.

- What can you hear?

CLASH! BASH!

Sometimes, you might hear the clash of antlers as male deer fight in the darkness.

SPLASH!

Can you hear fish swimming and leaping in a stream or river nearby?

CROAK! CROAK!

Male frogs croak, and all frogs might chirp and even make barking sounds.

CHIRP! CHIRP!

Crickets can chirp the whole night through.

TWIT-TWOO! TWIT-TWOO!

Owls hoot and screech in the dark of night.

Top tip: Use a recording or voice memo app on a smartphone to record sounds that you hear. Then you can play them back later to listen again or help identify the calls even when the animal has gone.

YAP! YAP!

Foxes are very active at night and yap and screech as they go about their business.

SNORT! SNUFFLE!

In some areas, voles snuffle along the ground.

Monday	Tuesday	Wednesday
Cricket (chirp) 8–9 pm	Frog (croak) 9 pm	Cricket (chirp) 8:15 pm
Owl (hoot) 10:15 pm	Owl (hoot) 10:15 pm	Frog (croak) 8:30 pm
		Cricket (chirp) 8:45 pm
		Fox (screech) 10:30 pm

RAINY DAYS

Don't let the rain spoil your holiday! There are plenty of **drizzly-day** activities to keep you busy at your campsite. Make your own board games, card games and activity sheets under a shelter to have fun with family and friends. Or, put on your wellies and **embrace the showers**!

CAMPERS 2+

COLOURING FUN

Colouring is a great way to keep busy, **slow down** and focus. **Create your own colouring sheets** for other campers to complete. Then ask them to make some for you too!

You will need
- A4 paper
- Pencil
- Black felt-tip pen
- Colouring pencils

Trace the picture on this page onto a blank piece of paper to get started!

Draw a camping scene or object on a piece of paper using your pencil.

When you are happy with your design, trace over the pencil lines with black felt-tip pen. Leave to dry. Then let your friends or family loose with their colouring pencils!

Make sure the white spaces are large enough for colouring in. Create big blocks of white space as simple images to colour. Try a more detailed design for older children and adults.

Colour by numbers

For an added challenge, design a colour-by-numbers activity.

1 = red
2 = blue
3 = yellow
4 = green
5 = brown

1 Create a key, showing a list of numbers and the colours they correspond to.

2 In each block of white space, write the number of the colour you'd like that area to be.

3 Pass the sheet to another camper to colour in. They must use the key to complete the picture.

Draw extra lines to break up large areas.

CAMPERS 2+

CAMPING QUEST

You will need
- 2 pieces of paper
- Felt-tip pens
- Objects to use as counters, such as stones, coins or seashells
- Glue (or sticky tape)

No space to pack a **board game**? No problem! Make your own, then **challenge** your friends and family to a match.

How to make

1 Draw your home in the bottom-left corner of one piece of paper. Label this 'START'.

2 Draw your campsite in the top-right corner. Label this 'FINISH'.

3 Draw a winding path from your home to the campsite. Divide it into spaces.

4 Write special instructions on some of the spaces, such as 'You read the map upside-down. Go back two spaces.'

5 Decorate the paper with your felt-tip pens. Finish the scene!

6 Trace the dice template from page 144 on to the other piece of paper. Write the numbers 1 to 6 on the different squares. Cut out, fold and glue into a cube shape.

You stop at a café for lunch. Miss a go!

Take a shortcut. Follow the arrow your next turn.

You forgot your tent. Go back to the start!

You could use a flattened piece of cardboard, such as a cereal box, for your game board.

Green light! Drive forwards 2 spaces!

START

CAMPERS 2+

CARD GAMES

Card games are a **classic pastime** for rainy days and cosy evenings. Make your own playing cards, and challenge an opponent to a **high-speed** game of Snap or a **brain-testing** match of Concentration.

How to make

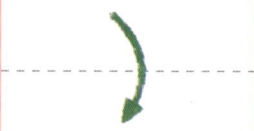

1 Lay one sheet of card on a flat surface, long side facing you. Fold it in half, bringing the top to the bottom. Crease, then open it out again.

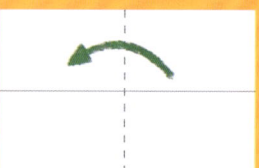

2 Fold the right edge to the left edge. Crease.

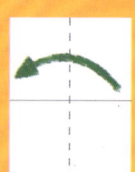

3 Fold the right edge to the left edge again. Crease.

4 Unfold the whole sheet. Cut along the creased lines. You should now have eight playing cards.

5 Repeat steps 1 to 4 twice, so that you have 24 cards in total.

6 Take two blank cards. Draw the same camping image, such as a tent, on each card.

7 Repeat for the remaining 11 pairs of cards, so you end up with 12 pairs of identical cards.

You will need
- 3 sheets of A4 card
- Scissors
- Felt-tip pens

"SNAP!"

SNAP!

How to play

1 Shuffle the cards all together.

2 Deal the cards evenly between two players, face down.

3 Begin the game with both players flipping over the top card from their pile at the same time. Place these side by side in the centre of the playing area. If the cards match, shout 'Snap!' The first person to say 'Snap' collects all the cards in the centre and places them at the bottom of their pile. If the cards do not match, play carries on.

4 Continue flipping cards together and yelling 'Snap' when they match. The game ends when one person has all the cards in their pile. They are the winner!

Flip faster and faster for a super-speedy snap-off! Who can keep their wits about them and spot a matching pair?

Whoops!
If a player calls out 'Snap!' when the cards DON'T match, he or she must give the top card from their pile to the other player.

CONCENTRATION

How to play

1 Shuffle the cards. Lay them face down on a flat surface in rows, to create a 4 x 6 grid of cards.

2 Take it in turns to turn over two cards. These could be any from the grid. If the cards are a matching pair, the player gets to keep them and take another turn. If the cards don't match, flip them back over, and play moves on to the next person.

3 Continue taking it in turns to flip over two cards at a time, trying to collect a match. When all the cards have been collected, the person with the most pairs wins.

Top tip!
Try to remember which card is which when they're flipped over to help you find matching pairs.

CAMPERS 1+

YOUR ANIMAL PERSONALITY

Take this quiz to discover which **animal you're most like**. Then take on the **mission** best suited to you. Try the quiz on your family and friends too. Do you all have different **animal personalities**?

1. What would you most like to be when you're grown up?
a. A teacher
b. A footballer
c. A scientist
d. An artist

2. Where would you prefer to live?
a. In the forest
b. In a busy city
c. At the top of a mountain
d. In a small town

3. The BEST Saturday would be spent...
a. Raising money for your favourite cause
b. Laughing with friends
c. Going to the library
d. Exploring nature

4. How would people describe you?
a. Confident
b. Hilarious
c. Serious
d. Sweet

5. In a group of friends, you...
a. Are the leader
b. Chat with everyone
c. Stick to yourself
d. Listen to people who need it

Mostly As
You are a bear! You are strong, steady and you like to lead and help others.
Your mission: Make up a rainy-day game for everyone to play!

Mostly Bs
You are a squirrel! You are playful, adaptable and happy to try new things.
Your mission: Tell funny jokes and make up stories to keep everyone happy.

Mostly Cs
You are a wolf! You are sharp, smart and happy to be alone, yet you form deep connections with people you trust.
Your mission: Lead your pack on a mindful walk in the rain. Ask everyone to walk quietly and notice the wild world around them.

Mostly Ds
You are a deer! You are gentle, graceful and sensitive.
Your mission: Set up a nature discovery walk. Ask everyone to choose an object they like from the walk. Listen as each person explains why they like that object.

CAMPERS 2+

ANIMAL GAMES

Get truly **in touch with nature** by being at one with the animals. Play **animal guessing games** and spend an afternoon acting like the **creatures around you**.

BEAR!

LION!

Animal acting
One person acts out an animal without saying a word. Everyone else must guess what the animal is. The first person to guess the correct answer acts out the next creature.

Animal sounds
One person must make the sound of an animal. Everyone else must guess the animal. The first person to guess correctly makes the next sound.

To increase the difficulty level, you could ask an adult to find clips of animal sounds on a mobile phone. Listen to the clip and see if anyone can name the noisy animal.

eEEOOorRRRr NNNNEeeeHHHhhh

COW!

DONKEY!

HORSE!

CRAB!

Animal boogie
Find a little bit of space under a shelter, or put on your wellies and raincoats and get out in the rain. Ask an adult to play music. Then ask the adult to call out different animal names. Each time they do, you must dance to the music in the style of that animal. Boogie like a baboon, slither like a snake and hop like a bunny!

ELEPHANT!

MONKEY!

107

CAMPERS 1+

NATURE YOGA

Find a flat space under a shelter and **reconnect with nature** to discover your **inner peace**. Try these nature-inspired **yoga poses**, then make up your own!

Mountain pose
Start your session with this strong pose to find your grounding. Stand with your feet about hip-width apart. Hold your arms out to the sides, palms facing forwards, to make a triangle mountain shape. Stand firm like a mountain, and take deep breaths as if you're breathing in energising mountain air.

Tree pose
Stand with your feet together. Slowly bring one leg up, turning out your knee and placing your foot flat on the inside of your other leg. Hold this pose for 10 seconds, taking deep breaths as you do. Focus on something in front of you to help keep your balance. Stand tall like a tree!

Butterfly

Sit on the ground, a cushion or a mat, and bring the soles of your feet together. Let your knees fall to the sides, and bring your feet in as close as you can. Flutter your knees up and down like a butterfly!

Beetle

Lie flat on your sleeping mat. Bring your knees in to your chest and grab hold of your feet. Stretch your legs up to the sky, as straight as you can. Wriggle around like a beetle on its back!

Invent your own!

Look outside your tent and make up your own moves based on the nature you see. Could you wind like a river? Stretch on all fours like a dog? What other poses could you try?

CAMPERS 2+

SPOTTING A–Z

Peer out through the tent window, or pop on some wellies, and **get spotting**! Use the **alphabet** to lead you through this **eye-catching** game.

How to play

1 The first player spots something around the campsite that starts with the letter A, such as ant. They point to it and say its name.

2 The next player must spot something with the letter B, such as barbecue. They point to it and say its name.

3 Continue taking it in turns to spot an item, going in order through the alphabet. If someone is stumped, they could be out of the game, or everyone else can help them out!

I SPY

Spot things around the campsite, and name them by their initial letter. For example, you could say, 'I spy with my little eye something beginning with S.' Everyone must shout out guesses until someone works out the word you have in mind. That person then spots the next item.

CAMPERS 1+ (PLUS ONE ADULT)

MUDDY KITCHEN

Step out into the mud and let your creativity **run wild**. Set up a **muddy kitchen** and make pretend cakes and potions with **natural ingredients**. Just remember not to **actually** taste them!

Note: Always make sure you have an adult's permission to use equipment for messy mud.

MUD CAKE

How to make and play

1 Put on your waterproof clothing and wellies. This will get messy!

2 Choose a baking tray or cooking pot.

3 Grab handfuls of mud and put them in the tray or pot as your pretend cake batter. Mix in stones, pinecones and anything else you like with a stick.

4 Dump out the mixture onto a plate. Shape it into a cake shape with your hands. Decorate it with leaves and flower petals.

5 Offer your pretend cake to your family!

WARNING! Never eat mud cake. It is not real food.

You will need
- Waterproof jacket and trousers
- Wellies
- Baking trays, pots and plates
- Natural items such as mud, sticks, dirt, leaves, stones, pinecones, flower petals
- Towel to dry off afterwards

Clean up! Make sure to scrub everything really well afterwards so there's no mud left on your pots and plates.

What's your recipe?
Try different combinations of 'ingredients' and different shapes for your cake. Have fun getting messy and creative in your muddy campground kitchen!

NATURAL POTIONS

You will need
- Waterproof jacket and trousers
- Wellies
- Rainwater
- Empty jar, such as a jam jar
- Wildflowers and leaves
- Stick
- Paper and pen
- Scissors
- Tape

WARNING! Never drink your concoctions.

How to make

Rose Kiss

1 Put on your waterproof clothing and wellies. Collect rainwater in your jar. Leave the jar outside until it is about half full of water. Keep the lid aside for later.

2 Add any natural items that you like, such as wildflowers or leaves. Use the stick to press these into the jar and mix them into the water. Place the lid on the jar.

3 Cut a small square of paper and write the name of your potion on it. Use the tape to attach it to the jar, making sure to completely cover the paper to keep it as waterproof as possible.

Perfume power
Do any of the materials you've found give off a scent? Try different combinations to create wild pretend perfumes.

CAMPERS 2+

SLIMY SPOTTING

You will need
- Notepad
- Pen
- Waterproof jacket and trousers
- Wellies
- Magnifying glass (optional; see page 84 to make your own)

Some creepy-crawlies **love the rain**! Slip on your wellies and go out **into the drizzle**, just like these slimy creatures do. How many **can you spot**?

How to make and play

1 Draw six vertical lines on your notepad.

2 At the top of the second column, write 'Slugs'. At the top of the third column, write 'Snails'. At the top of the fourth column, write 'Worms'. At the top of the final column, write 'Frogs'.

3 Draw enough rows underneath for each person taking part. Write their names in the first column.

4 Put on your waterproofs and head into the great outdoors! Look carefully for any creeping creatures. Whenever someone spots one, add a mark on the tally chart.

5 When you're back under shelter, count up each total. Who saw the most slugs? Snails? Worms? Frogs?

Be an observer
What are the creatures doing in the rain? Are they finding shelter, or are they on the move? How do they get around? Note any other creatures that you spot too. What comes out to play on a rainy day?

	Slugs	Snails	Worms	Frogs
Dad	III	I	II	I
Uncle Az	II	IIII	II	
Joey	IIII	II	III	II
Lillia		I	II	IIII II
Eli	IIII	II	I	I

CAMPERS 1+

RAINDROP MUSIC

You will need
- Waterproof jacket and trousers
- Wellies
- Pots and pans
- Tins and jars

Have you ever stopped to **listen to the rain**? Can you **make music** by imitating the tinkly sound of the rain on various items around your campsite?

Listen to the sound the rain makes on different surfaces. How does it sound when it lands on the roof of your tent? In a puddle? On the barbecue lid?

TINK TINK

PITTER PATTER

TIP TAP

Copy the sounds of the rain. Tap out the patterns you hear with a spoon.

Can you lay out different items to create a symphony with the different sounds working together?

PLOP SPLASH PLOP

Place different items out in the rain. Try pots and pans, full tins, empty tins, glass jars... How does the rain sound on each? Tinkly or more of a plop? With a high pitch or low?

Note: Never do this activity if there is any thunder or lightning!

CAMPERS 1+

MAKE A RAIN STICK

You will need
- Empty kitchen towel roll
- Paper or card
- Pencil
- Scissors
- Tape
- Aluminium foil
- 4 tablespoons of rice
- Felt-tip pens

Join in with the sound of the rain. Make your own **rain stick** and tip it back and forth to hear a gentle swishing sound like raindrops. It's **raining fun**!

How to make and play

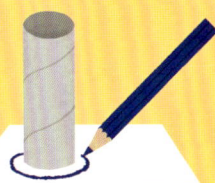

1 Stand the kitchen towel roll on the piece of paper or card. Draw a circle on the card around the end of the roll, about 1 cm (0.5 in) out from the roll. Cut this out.

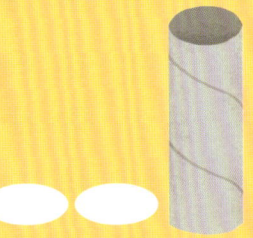

2 Trace the circle on the remaining card and cut out. You should now have two circles.

3 Wrap one circle over one end of the kitchen towel roll. To help with this, cut notches in the edge, as shown. Tape in place.

This slows down the rice to help make the rain sound.

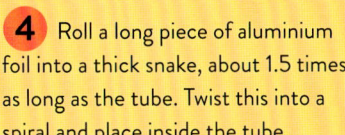

4 Roll a long piece of aluminium foil into a thick snake, about 1.5 times as long as the tube. Twist this into a spiral and place inside the tube.

5 Hold the tube sealed side down. Carefully pour the rice into the tube, keeping it upright.

6 Wrap the other circle over the open end of the tube, in the same way as step 3. Tape securely in place.

7 Decorate your rain stick with felt-tip pens if you like.

8 Slowly tip the rain stick back and forth and listen to the sound of the rain!

Use your rain stick inside so it doesn't get soggy in the real rain!

CAMPERS 1+ (PLUS ONE ADULT)

PUDDLE JUMPING

You will need
- Waterproof jacket and trousers
- Wellies
- Large umbrella
- Small stones
- Leaves and twigs
- Towel to dry off afterwards

Never be afraid to **dance in the rain**! Jump, twirl and play in the puddles. Try these **puddle-tastic** moves and challenges to get you started.

Rain dance
It's a dance party... puddle style! Take your dance moves outside and try them right in the middle of a puddle. Kick the water and splash as you dance back and forth. Can you spin in the centre of the puddle?

Froggy jump
Jump across a puddle like a frog. What other creatures could you be to play in the rain?

Umbrella partner
Grab an umbrella and use it as your dance partner. Leave it closed and use it like a walking stick. Place the point down on the ground and twirl around it. Then, open the umbrella above your head and spin!

Biggest splash
Ask another camper to join in. Count to three then jump into two side-by-side puddles. Who can make the biggest splash? Now try tossing small stones into the puddles. Who can make the largest splash with these?

Highest jump
Take it in turns running and jumping into a puddle. Who can jump the highest? Try out different landings to make different splashes. Will you land strongly on two feet, or skip across?

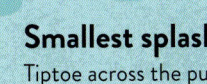

Smallest splash
Tiptoe across the puddle and make as few splashes as possible. Who can make the tiniest ripples?

Note: Always check with an adult that the puddles are safe to jump in.

Float or sink?
Try resting natural items such as leaves or twigs on big puddles. Do they float or sink?

119

AROUND THE CAMPFIRE

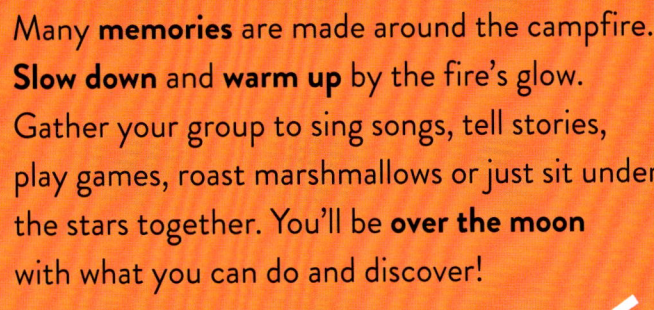

Many **memories** are made around the campfire. **Slow down** and **warm up** by the fire's glow. Gather your group to sing songs, tell stories, play games, roast marshmallows or just sit under the stars together. You'll be **over the moon** with what you can do and discover!

CAMPERS 1+ (PLUS ONE ADULT)

MARSHMALLOW DELIGHTS

Cook food on **your very own campfire**. See pages 22–23 to get a fire going, then make some marshmallow delicacies. Go on, **treat yourself**!

ROAST MARSHMALLOWS

You will need
- Stick or toasting fork
- Marshmallows
- Campfire

Make sure the stick goes all the way through the marshmallow.

How to make

1 Carefully push a marshmallow onto the end of the stick or toasting fork. Watch your fingers!

2 Gripping the other end of the stick, hold the marshmallow just above the fire (but not touching it).

3 Turn the stick slowly so that the marshmallow cooks evenly.

4 Remove the stick from the fire when the marshmallow is golden all the way around. Leave for at least one minute before tasting. It will be hot!

WARNING! Always have an adult around when cooking on the campfire.

Top toasting tips
- Choose a stick that is at least as long as an adult's arm. Rub another stick against it to smooth and clean it.
- Wait for the flames to die down before toasting your marshmallow. Big flames will just burn it.
- If you do get a burnt black layer on your marshmallow, don't worry! Once it's cool, you can peel off this layer. Discard it in the fire, and eat the gooey goodness that's left inside!

S'MORES

You will need
- Squares of chocolate
- Plain biscuits
- Plate or napkin
- Stick
- Marshmallows
- Campfire

How to make

1 Lay a square of chocolate on a plain biscuit. Place on a plate or napkin, ready for later.

2 Place a marshmallow on a stick. Roast the marshmallow over the campfire. Turn it slowly to cook it evenly.

BE CAREFUL! Remember, the marshmallow will be hot.

3 Using the stick, place the marshmallow on the chocolate on the biscuit. Carefully place another biscuit on top of the marshmallow, to create a small sandwich.

4 Press down gently on the top biscuit and slowly slide the stick out of the marshmallow.

5 Let the heat from the marshmallow melt the chocolate. Once it is cool enough to eat, devour and enjoy!

Layer up your ingredients for a super-indulgent treat!

Did you know?
The name 's'more' comes from the words 'some more'. Will you be asking for more once you've had your first taste?

CAMPERS 4+

CAMPFIRE GAMES

Once you're sitting in a circle **around the campfire**, you're in prime position for some **fun party games**. Play and **giggle** the night away!

WHISPERS

How to play

1 One person thinks of a funny phrase or sentence, such as 'She sells seashells by the seashore.'

2 That person whispers it into the ear of the camper sitting to their left.

3 That camper then whispers whatever they heard into the ear of the next camper in the circle.

4 Carry on whispering the message around the circle, until it reaches the last camper (the one just before the person who started the message).

5 The last camper announces out loud whatever they heard. This might have changed quite a lot as it got passed around the circle! For example, they might have heard the message morph into 'She smells bee spells by the sea snore!'

NUMBERS

How to play

The aim of this game is to count as a group to 100. Simple, right? Not quite! The catch is that there's no specific order of people speaking, and you can't communicate with each other, either. No talking or pointing!

One person begins the game by saying 'one'. Anyone else can jump in with the next number in the sequence, and as many more numbers as they like. But as soon as two people say the same number at the same time, you must start back at 1. How far can you get?

SOUNDS

How to play

1. One person in the circle names a letter sound, such as 'm' or 'th'.

2. Going around the circle one at a time, each camper must say a word beginning with that letter sound.

3. When someone can't think of a word, that sound is finished. The next person in the circle thinks up a new sound, and you can go around again!

Rhythm clap

Add a time challenge to up the ante with this game. As a group, use your hands to mark a rhythm. Pat your knees twice, then clap. Repeat this rhythm as you go around the circle. Try to get each person to say their word on the clap.

CAMPERS 2+

CAMPFIRE SONGS

Relax and **sing your heart out** by the warmth of the fire. Try these campfire **song games** to get going!

DOWN BY THE BAY

This classic song is yours to fill in! Start with the standard lyric, and then add your own lines.

How silly can you get?

Down by the bay,
Where the watermelons grow,
Back to my home,
I dare not go.
For if I do,
My mother will say...
Have you ever seen a ___ ___-ing ___?
Down by the bay!

Fill in the gaps on this line!

Choose two rhyming words and include an action word in the middle.

For example:
Have you ever seen a bear wearing underwear?
Have you ever seen a pig dancing a jig?
Have you ever seen a dragon pulling a wagon?
Have you ever seen a fox wearing spotty socks?

NAME THAT TUNE

One person hums or whistles the first line of a song. Can anyone name that tune? If someone has a musical instrument, such as a guitar, even better! Ask them to play part of the song and see if anyone can join in.

HAPPY BIRTHDAY?

HMMM HMMMMMM HMM HMMM

OLD MACDONALD?

Team tunes

You could divide into teams for this game. One team hums a song together, while the other team must guess what it is. Set a time limit, such as one minute per song. If the other team can guess correctly before the time is up, they win a point! Take it in turns humming a song for the other team. The first team to reach 10 points wins!

If You're Happy and You Know It

Head, Shoulders, Knees and Toes

Row, Row, Row Your Boat

Song prompts

If you're stumped for tunes, ask everyone to write the names of some well-known songs on small pieces of paper. Place all of these into a hat. Each person must take one piece of paper out of the hat and hum or whistle that song for others to guess the title.

Twinkle, Twinkle Little Star

CAMPERS 3+

TELLING TALES

Telling tales around the campfire goes back centuries. Join in the **tradition** and make up your own **spectacular stories**.

TEAM TALE

Work together to tell a tale. One person starts the story with a sentence. The person to their left adds another sentence. Carry on around the circle, with each camper adding one line to the story until it's done. Where will the story go, and how will it end?

THAT TIME WHEN...

How to make and play

1 Tear a piece of paper into small pieces. Each person writes a story idea on a piece of paper, starting with 'Tell a story about a time when...'.

2 Put all the pieces of paper into a hat.

3 The oldest person in the circle goes first. They reach into the hat and pull out one piece of paper at random. They must then tell the story from that prompt. They can talk about a time when this thing happened in real life, or make up a wild story from their imagination!

4 Make your way around the circle, with each person pulling out one story idea and telling a story as they go.

Tell a story about a time when you went camping.

Tell a story about a time when you were caught in the rain.

Tell a story about a time when you bumped into someone who looked exactly like you.

Tell a story about a time when you went to space.

SPOOKY STORIES

Try these tips to spin a spooky tale. Just make sure everyone is happy to hear it!

- Start off by saying you heard the story from someone you know. This makes it feel more believable.

- Speak slowly and take long pauses. Everyone should be super silent listening to what comes next.

- Use a louder voice to make people jump!

- Use sound effects, such as crunching the leaves below your feet or tapping on your chair.

- Lean in, and shine your flashlight on your face, holding it up from your chin.

- Finish with a funny ending!

Aim to make your story spooky, but not too scary. You want people to be able to sleep at night. Make sure everyone knows it's just made up!

CAMPERS 2+

STORYTELLING STONES

Make your own **storytelling stones** to help get your **creative juices flowing**. What **crazy tales** can you spin?

You will need
- At least 12 small, smooth stones
- Paint and paintbrushes
- Permanent markers
- 3 containers, such as bags, snack pots or boxes

How to make

1 Divide the stones into three piles of four.

2 Paint a different character on each of the first four stones, such as a cat, a unicorn, an astronaut and a chef.

3 On each of the next four stones, write an action word, such as 'flying', 'swimming', 'dancing' and 'sailing'.

4 On the last four stones, paint four different objects, such as a key, a house, a hat and a treasure chest.

5 Place the groups of stones in three separate bags, snack pots or boxes. Label each bag or box as 'Character', 'Action' and 'Object'.

Decorate more stones for each category if you'd like even more story options!

Paint your stones in the daytime, ready to use around the campfire in the evening.

How to play

1 The storyteller takes one stone from each bag or box: a character stone, an action-word stone and an object stone.

2 They must then tell a story using the three stones as inspiration. Perhaps an astronaut enters a dance competition to try to win treasure? Or a cat in a funny hat goes sailing? See where the stones take you!

3 Once the first person has told their tale, place the stones back in their corresponding bags or boxes. Let another camper have a turn! What combination of stones will they draw out?

Camping and more
Make your stones camping themed, such as an explorer, 'canoeing' and a tent, or go wilder with your ideas. It's up to you!

THE EXPLORER WENT CANOEING AND CAME ACROSS A STRANGE TENT...

CAMPERS 4+

GUESS WHO

You will need
- Sticky notes (one for each person in the game), or small pieces of paper and tape
- Felt-tip pens

Take on a **secret identity**... then see if you can work out who you are! Take turns asking questions to the group to **guess who** as you sit and ponder around the campfire.

How to make and play

1 Sit in a circle around the campfire. Get each person to secretly write the name of a well-known book, TV or movie character on a sticky note.

2 Each person places their sticky note on the forehead of the camper to their left, making sure that the camper doesn't see what it says.

3 The oldest player goes first. They ask the group a yes or no question about their character, such as 'Am I a girl?'

4 The rest of the campers can answer 'yes' or 'no' (or 'don't know'). If they answer 'yes', the player can ask another question. If they answer 'no' or 'don't know', move on to the next person.

5 Going clockwise around the circle, take it in turns to ask one yes or no question at a time to the group. If you think you know who your character is, make that your question on your next turn, such as 'Am I Prince Charming?'

6 When you've guessed correctly, you're done! Stay in the game to help answer questions for anyone remaining.

CAMPERS 4+ (PLUS ONE ADULT)

TORCH GAMES

You will need
- One torch per player
- An adult to supervise

Stand up from your cosy campfire seat to play these games **under the cover of darkness** at your campsite. Grab a **torch** and stay safe!

SLEEPING BUNNIES

Try this night-time twist on the classic party game.

How to play

1 Choose one person to hold the torch. They are the explorer. Everyone else is a tired bunny.

2 While the explorer closes their eyes and counts to 20, all the bunnies must lie down on the ground and turn their torches off.

3 The explorer then carefully wanders around the campsite, using their torch to cast a light on the ground. When they shine a light on a sleeping bunny, that person must try to stay as still as possible – they can only breathe and blink!

4 Without touching the players, the explorer can try to make the bunnies move, such as by making funny noises or telling jokes. If a bunny moves, they're out. They can then use their torch to help the explorer.

5 The last person lying still on the ground is the winner. They become the explorer in the next round!

STILL AS A STATUE

Stay standing in this statuesque variation!

How to play

1 Pretend that your campground is a fancy garden. Choose one person to be the groundskeeper. They hold a torch. Choose one more person to be a visitor. Everyone else will be a statue.

2 The groundskeeper and visitor close their eyes and count to 20. While they do, the statues must strike a pose, then freeze!

3 The groundskeeper and visitor open their eyes. The groundskeeper then leads the visitor on a tour, using their torch to show off the 'fancy garden'.

4 When the torch lands on a statue, that person must not move at all! The groundskeeper can tell jokes, pull funny faces and more to try to make the statues move, without touching them.

5 If a statue moves, they become another visitor. The last statue standing is the winner.

WARNING! Never shine a torch directly in someone's eyes.

MORE TORCH FUN

Don't want to stop the torch-tastic fun? Try these other ideas:

Torch limbo
Shine the torch straight across in the dark to create a horizontal beam. Take turns ducking under it, just like limbo. Lower the torch with each turn. How low can you go without breaking the beam?

Torch dance party
Play some party music and dance with your torches. They will flash around like a disco ball! Just be sure to keep the music to a low volume if there are other campers nearby.

Torch art
Take it in turns using a torch to draw pictures or letters in the air. Can anyone guess what you've drawn?

CAMPERS 3+

SHADOW THEATRE

You will need
- Pencil
- Black card
- Scissors
- Ice lolly sticks
- Tape
- Tent
- Torch

Use your tent, a torch and your imagination for **fireside fun**. Make some **puppets**, then **put on a show**!

How to make

1 Draw characters and objects onto the black card.

2 Cut out the shapes.

3 Tape an ice lolly stick to the back of each shape. You now have your shadow puppets.

How to play

1 Wait until it is dark outside. Have your audience sit outside the tent, facing its side.

2 Ask a helper to sit inside the tent with you, holding a torch towards the tent's wall.

3 Hold your puppets in the light, between the torch and the tent's wall. These will show up as shadows to your audience on the other side.

4 Put on a show!

HURRAH!

What's your story?
Think of a story that you'll tell with your puppets. You could perform a favourite fairy tale or make up a story of your own. Think about the characters that you'll need. You could cut out objects such as houses or trees too.

Hands only
Instead of using card and sticks, you can make shapes with your hands to look like different animals. Move them in the beam of light to create shadows on the wall of the tent.

Try these to get started:

Crocodile

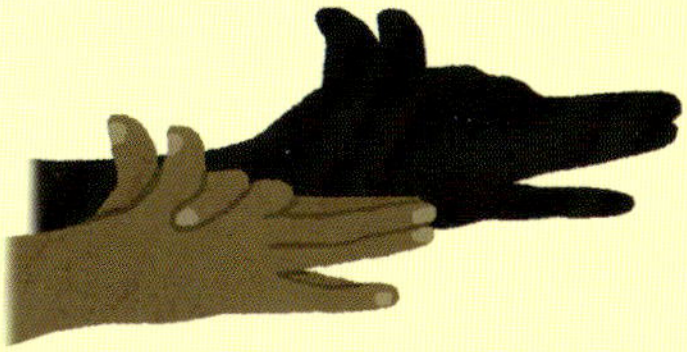

Dog

Rabbit

THE END!

AGAIN!

Zoom in or out
Move the torch closer to your hands to make the shadows bigger. Move it farther away for smaller shapes.

KNOW THE NIGHT SKY

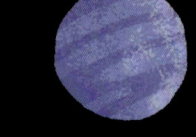

How well do you know the **night sky**? Lean back on a clear night and spend some time with the **darkness** above. What can you discover?

MOMENT WITH THE MOON

The Moon is our closest neighbour in space. How well do you know your neighbour?

Phases of the Moon

As the Moon orbits around Earth, we see it lit up in the sky. Over one lunar month (about 29 days), it appears to change shape in the sky, based on what we can see. Look at the phases of the Moon below. Then look at the Moon in the sky above you when you're camping. Can you work out which phase you're seeing?

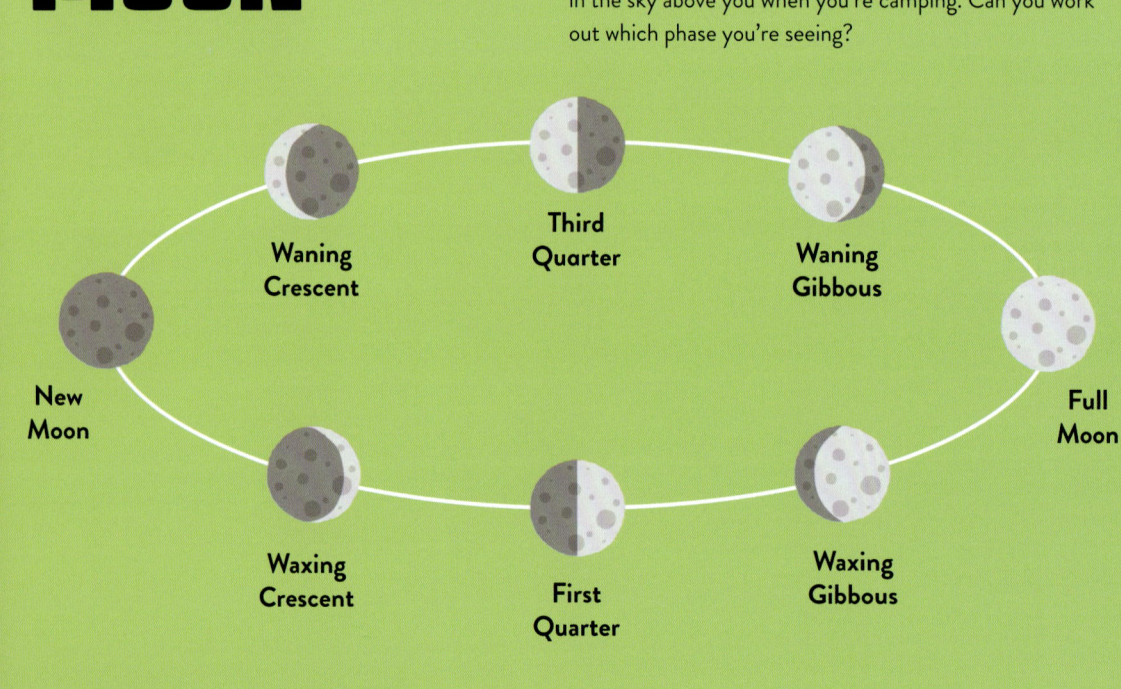

PLANET, SATELLITE OR STAR?

There are many other objects to spot in the night sky. Do you know how to tell them apart? Look for these bright lights:

Look closer...
The Moon is covered in light and shadows. Use binoculars, if you have some, to look closer. Can you spot craters made by impacts of asteroids and comets? Look out also for dark areas on the Moon. These were formed by volcanic eruptions and are known as mares (meaning 'seas') because people once thought they were full of water (but we know now that they're not!). What can you see on the Moon?

Satellite
Satellites move slowly and steadily across the sky. They are human-made objects that orbit Earth. Look for the International Space Station as it passes by. Unlike an aeroplane, it won't have any blinking lights.

Star
Stars twinkle in the sky, and shooting stars move quickly. Turn the page to find out more about stars and the patterns they make in the night sky.

Planet
A planet doesn't twinkle in the sky. Its light shines solid. Some of them appear very bright or have a slight colour to them. If you see a pale red dot, it could be Mars! Look at apps and online to find out which planets you might be able to see from your location and at what time of year.

KEEP A LOG
Take photos or draw sketches of the Moon and the night sky each night of your camping trip. How does it change over the time you're there?

CAMPERS 1+

GAZE AT THE STARS

You will need
- Blanket
- Clear dark night

The open air, away from city lights, is the **perfect place** for staring at the stars. Lie down, get comfy, let your eyes adjust and **watch the stars** reveal themselves to you.

Lay a blanket on the ground and lie flat on your back. Look up at the night sky.

We see our galaxy, the Milky Way, as a cloudy band of stars.

Constellations

Long ago, people grouped stars into patterns called constellations. They told stories about these patterns and named them based on the object or character the pattern resembled. Can you spot any famous constellations?

Orion

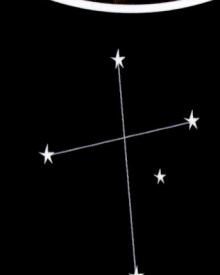
Southern Cross (Crux)

Northern hemisphere

Southern hemisphere

Where in the world

The night sky looks different depending on where and when you're looking at it from. You will see different stars in the northern and southern hemispheres, and in spring, summer, autumn and winter. Check a stargazing app or website to find out which constellations you can see from your campsite.

Shooting stars

Shooting stars can be hard to spot, but there are certain times of the year when a meteor shower brings lots of streaking lights in one night. Check online to find out if there are any meteor showers expected during your camping holiday. Make a wish if you see a shooting star!

Make up your own!

Look at the stars above you at this very moment. What patterns and pictures can you see? Join the dots in the sky and make up names for your constellations. You could tell tales of the creatures too. Why are they in the sky? How did they get there? What do they mean?

Friendly competition

Up the stakes by introducing an element of competition. Lie down with your family and friends. Who can spot the first shooting star? Who can count the most planets or constellations? Keep track in a logbook.

ENDLESS FUN!

The great outdoors is a never-ending source of **discovery and fun.** Look around you and see what activities and games you can **dream up.** What could you do with a pinecone and a stick? What games can you play by the fire? What inspiration can you take from the birds and creatures by your campsite? Try these ideas to **get you going**...

Look up more recipes for cooking on a campfire. Learn how to make a jacket potato by wrapping it in foil!

Play noughts and crosses, camping style. Make a grid from sticks and use stones for noughts and pinecones for crosses.

Find a deck of cards or a board game and play games with your family and friends. Turn over to page 144 to learn how to make your own dice.

Cut out star or triangle shapes from card and paint them. Poke small holes into the shapes and thread them onto a long piece of string. Hang this around your campsite to create magical woodland bunting. Just remember to take it all down before you go home.

Carry out a photoshoot with the great outdoors as your backdrop. Think up fun and funny family poses!

WHAT OTHER ACTIVITIES CAN YOU THINK UP?

MAKE YOUR OWN DICE

When a game calls for it, use this **template** to make a dice out of paper.

1 Place a piece of paper over this page. Trace the template onto your piece of paper.

2 Write a number from 1 to 6 in each square on your paper.

3 Cut out along the solid lines. Fold on the dashed lines to create a cube shape.

4 Use glue or sticky tape to secure the tabs in place.

You can use digits, dots or even stars to show the numbers on your dice. Make it your own!

Photo Credits

The publisher would like to thank the following for their kind permission to reproduce their photographs in this book:
Key: t=top; b=bottom; c=centre; r=right, l=left, bg=background

Elzani Smit: 10 b, 17 tr, 52 cl, 52 br, 66 b, 95 t, 105 t, 129 br

Duck Egg Blue Limited: 32 r, 38 b, 39 t, 65 b, back cover tl

Laura Baker: 109 bl, 109 br

Alamy: Hero Images Inc. 3 cr, 120 b, 125 tr

Getty Images: Westend61 / Rosa Hellregen 10 tl, 19 br; Ariel Skelley/Blend Images LLC 23 b, back cover tc; bearacreative91 c

Shutterstock.com: saltodemata 3 br, 54 b, 74-75; Jacob Lund 3 cl, 47 b; Tatevosian Yana 3 bl, 81 tr, cover tr; Julian Popov 7 br, 43 br; all_about_people 7 bc, 43 bc, cover bl; perfectlab 7 tl, 98 b, 115 t; katarinag 9 bc, 74 t; Elena Chevalier 9 tr, 61 c; Photo Volcano 10 r, 29 b; VP Photo Studio 13 br; wavebreakmedia 15 b, 50 cl; Maria Symchych 16 tr, back cover tr; James Aloysius Mahan V 17 bl; Pixel-Shot 27 bl, 98 tl, 113 t, 134 t; ANDREI_SITURN 28 t; Perfect Angle Images 32 tl, 41 cl; PeopleImages.com - Yuri A 32 b, 46 b; fizkes 35 b; LightField Studios 41 b; Mariia Boiko 50 tr; Lordn 50 cb; Mirko Graul 53 br; Anna LoFi 54 tl, 57 bl, 57 br; STUDIO GRAND WEB 54 r, 61 tl; Igor Nikushin 57 c; Zzzenia 58 c; Pressmaster 59 t; pepsun2013 61 tr; AnnaKoro 65 tr; Janine C 65 tl; Megan Czarnocki 65 c; VasitChaya 68 t; rbkomar 73 br; Bembo20 74 bl, cover tr; AdaCo 74; Oxik 75 tl; Halfpoint 76 b, 87 t; In Green 76 tl, 89 tl; Irelee 76 r, 78 r; ninii 85 tr; Breaking The Walls 85 cr; Axel jahnke 85 bl; Lirtlon S 85 tl; Jolanta Wojcicka 85 br; BalanceFormCreative 86 b; prapann 89 tr; kezza 89 c; Roman Samborskyi 91 cr; Marina Demidiuk 93 b; narikan 98 r, 119 b; Alinute Silzeviciute 107 t; Olena Kosynska 108 t; adriaticfoto 110 b; FotoHelin 112 t; Dmitry Naumov 120 r, 137 b; Olesia Bilkei 120 tl, 126 t; oliveromg 122 c; EvgeniiAnd 123 br; Nata Bene 123 bl; Irina Starikova3432 130 b; michaeljung 133 b; Janon Stock 139 br; anatoliy_gleb 140 c; Nata_marc 142 tr; Evgeny Atamanenko 142 bl, 143 bl; Didecs 143 bg